THE
★ GREAT ★
SOCIETY

Also by Robert Schenkkan

All the Way

The Kentucky Cycle

By the Waters of Babylon

The Marriage of Miss Hollywood and King Neptune

Handler

Four One-Act Plays

The Dream Thief

Heaven on Earth

Final Passages

A Single Shard

The Devil and Daniel Webster

THE
★ GREAT ★
SCIETY

ROBERT SCHENKKAN

Grove Press
New York

Published simultaneously in Canada
Printed in the United States of America

The Great Society was developed, in part, with assistance from the Orchard Project, a program of The Exchange (www.exchangenyc.org)

First edition published by Grove Atlantic: May 2017

ISBN 978-0-8021-2373-2
eISBN 978-0-8021-9136-6

FIRST EDITION

Grove Press
an imprint of Grove Atlantic
154 West 14th Street
New York, NY 10011

Distributed by Publishers Group West

groveatlantic.com

17 18 19 20   10 9 8 7 6 5 4 3 2 1

For those extraordinary men and women who fought so hard and sacrificed so much in the fight for Civil Rights.

THE
★ GREAT ★
SOCIETY

PRODUCTION CREDITS

The Great Society was commissioned by the Seattle Repertory Theatre and developed by the Oregon Shakespeare Festival for their American Revolutions: The United States History Cycle, a ten-year program of up to thirty-seven new plays about moments of change in United States History. It received its world premiere at the Oregon Shakespeare Festival on July 27, 2014. The production was directed by Bill Rauch. Bill Rauch, Artistic Director; Cynthia Rider, Executive Director; Christopher Acebo, Scenic Design; Deborah M. Dryden, Costume Design; David Weiner, Lighting Design; Shawn Sagady, Video Design; Paul James Prendergast, Composer & Sound Design; Tom Bryant, Dramaturgy; U. Jonathan Toppo, Fight Director; Rebecca Clark Carey, Voice and Text Director. The production sponsors were the Edgerton Foundation New Play Award, and Charlotte Lin and Robert P. Porter. The production partners were The Paul G. Allen Family Foundation, Trine Sorensen and Michael Jacobson, Kevin and Suzanne Kahn, and The Kinsman Foundation.

The cast was as follows:

Lyndon Baines Johnson	Jack Willis
Appel/Daley/Wheeler	Denis Arndt
Dr. Martin Luther King Jr.	Kenajuan Bentley
Stokely Carmichael/Lewis	Wayne T. Carr
Bobby Kennedy/Ens.	Danforth Comins
J. Edgar Hoover/Ens.	Richard Elmore
Hubert Humphrey/Ens.	Peter Frechette

Wallace/Nixon/McCone	Jonathan Haugen
Dirksen/DeLoach/Ens.	Michael J. Hume
Moses/Williams/Frye/Ens.	Kevin Kenerly
Coretta Scott King/Ens.	Bakesta King
Lady Bird Johnson/Ens.	Terri McMahon
McNamara/Mills/Ens.	Mark Murphey
Pat Nixon/Muriel Humphrey	Rachael Warren
Abernathy/Powell/Ens.	Tyrone Wilson
Bevel/Jackson/Ens.	Tobie Windham
Walinsky/Westmoreland/Ens.	Rex Young

The Great Society received its Washington premiere at the Seattle Repertory Theatre on November 14, 2014. The production was directed by Bill Rauch. Jerry Manning, Artistic Director; Benjamin Moore, Managing Director; Christopher Acebo, Scenic Design; Deborah M. Dryden, Costume Design; David Weiner, Lighting Design; Shawn Sagady, Video Design; Paul James Prendergast, Composer & Sound Design; Tom Bryant, Dramaturgy; Sarah Smith, Associate Costume Design; U. Jonathan Toppo, Fight Director; Nicole A. Watson, Associate Director; Rebecca Clark Carey, Voice and Text Director.

The cast was as follows:

Rev. Martin Luther King Jr.	Kenajuan Bentley
Stokely Carmichael/John Lewis/Ensemble	Wayne Carr
Sen. Robert F. Kennedy/Charles Robb/Ensemble	Danforth Comins
J. Edgar Hoover/Ensemble	Richard Elmore
Vice President Hubert Humphrey/Ensemble	Peter Frechette
Gov. George Wallace/Sherriff Jim Clark/Richard M. Nixon/ John McCone/Norman Morrison/Ensemble	Jonathan Haugen
Sen. Everett Dirksen/"Deke" DeLoach/Colonel Al Lingo/Clark Clifford/Ensemble	Michael J. Hume
James Bevel/Jimmie Lee Jackson/Ensemble	Reginald André Jackson
Bob Moses/Rev. Dobynes/Hosea Williams/Marquette Frye/Ensemble	Kevin Kenerly
Sally Childress/Coretta Scott King/Ensemble	Bakesta King
Lady Bird Johnson/Ensemble	Terri McMahon
Robert McNamara/Rep. Wilbur Mills/Ensemble	Mark Murphey

Adam Walinsky/General William Westmoreland/
Seymore Trammel/Stanley Levison/
Gardner Ackley/Ensemble   Michael Patten

Sherriff's Auxiliary/Muriel Humphrey/
Lynda Bird Johnson/Pat Nixon/Ensemble Caroline Shaffer

President Lyndon Baines Johnson   Jack Willis

Rev. Ralph Abernathy/Rep. Adam Clayton Powell/
Ensemble   Tyrone Wilson

Dr. James Z. Appel/Richard J. Daley/
General Earle Wheeler/Ensemble   Michael Winters

CHARACTERS

LBJ   President Lyndon Baines Johnson

VICE PRESIDENT HUBERT HUMPHREY

SENATOR EVERETT DIRKSEN   Senate Minority Leader (GOP)

SENATOR BOBBY KENNEDY

ADAM WALINSKY   Aide to Senator Kennedy

MLK   Dr. Martin Luther King, Head of SCLC

REPRESENTATIVE ADAM CLAYTON POWELL   (D) Secretary

J. EDGAR HOOVER   Head of the FBI

DEKE DELOACH   Aide to Hoover

ROBERT MCNAMARA   Secretary of Defense

BOB MOSES   Founder and Head of SNCC

STOKELY CARMICHAEL   SNCC Organizer

RALPH ABERNATHY   MLK's close friend. SCLC

SHERIFF JIM CLARK   Sheriff of Dallas County, Alabama

REVEREND DOBYNES   Minister Marion, Alabama

JIMMIE LEE JACKSON   Church Deacon in Marion, Ala.

CORETTA KING   wife of MLK

GENERAL WESTMORELAND   Head of American forces in Vietnam

PRESIDENT APPEL   American Medical Association

LADY BIRD JOHNSON   wife of LBJ

SHERIFF'S AUXILIARY White woman volunteer for Sheriff Clark

HOSEA WILLIAMS SNCC Organizer

JAMES BEVEL SCLC Organizer

JOHN LEWIS SNCC Organizer

COLONEL AL LINGO Head of the Alabama State Police

GOVERNOR GEORGE WALLACE Governor of Alabama

SEYMORE TRAMMEL Aide to Governor Wallace

JOHN MCCONE Head of the CIA

GARDNER ACKLEY Council of Economic Advisors

MURIEL HUMPHREY wife of Hubert Humphrey

REPORTER#1

REPORTER#2

REPORTER#3

RONALD FRYE Former US Airman

CHP#1

CHP#2

FEMALE RIOTER#1

MALE RIOTER#1

MALE RIOTER#2

MAYOR RICHARD DALEY Mayor of Chicago

RICHARD NIXON Former Vice President

REPRESENTATIVE WILBUR MILLS (D) Chairman, House Ways and Means Committee

NORMAN MORRISON Quaker anti-war protester

REPORTERS

NEWSCASTER

GENERAL WHEELER

CLARK CLIFFORD   Secretary of Defense

VARIOUS
AIDES, TROOPERS, CROWD, MARCHERS, REPORTERS, RIOTERS,
BLACK MOURNERS etc.

SETTINGS

Congress

Oval Office, White House

Senator Bobby Kennedy's Office

J. Edgar Hoover's Office, FBI Headquarters

Outside Brown Chapel, Selma, Alabama

Hotel Room, Selma, Alabama

A street. Marion, Alabama

Living Room, Humphrey House, Washington

Steps of State Capitol, Montgomery, Alabama

Near Pettus Bridge, Selma, Alabama

Pettus Bridge

Rose Garden, White House

Briefing Room, White House

Theater, White House

Hallway, White House

Floor of the Senate

President's Room, Senate

Avalon Blvd. Watts, LA

Hotel Room, Chicago

Gage Park, Chicago

House of Representatives

Senate

SCLC Headquarters

Hotel Hallway, Anaheim, CA

Hallway, White House

PRODUCTION NOTES

Same setting as for ALL THE WAY. A wooden raked playing area. On both sides are "bull-pens," slightly recessed areas with wooden benches, chairs, props, costume pieces, etc, where the acting company, the WITNESSES, *wait in full view of the audience until they enter the playing area.*

The Witnesses are not "in character" while they wait but they are very much attentive to the action of the play until they enter the scene. Witnesses may play several parts except for the actor playing LBJ.

Upstage Center is an enormous screen divided into several smaller screens as if you had stacked a series of Televisions one on top of the other. This is the electronic TALLY BOARD (TB) for votes as well as a screen for live images broadcast directly from the stage, archival newsreel footage, statistics, maps, super-titles, etc.

Through the course of the action, the set should be broken down and "damaged." By the very end of the play, ideally a set of stairs or risers Stage Center, should have been constructed out of the debris of the original set.

Scenes should always move quickly, flowing one into another, and never stopping to settle.

ACT ONE

SPOT up on **LBJ** *standing Center Stage. The* **WITNESSES** *enter, chanting, "All the way with LBJ!" The chant builds to a crescendo, and cuts off. LBJ speaks directly to the audience.*

LBJ One year when he was feelin' flush, my daddy took us all to the rodeo. Boiled peanuts, big dill pickles the size of your fist and pink cotton candy for the kids; for the adults, Shiner beer topped off with a snort of home-brew from a pocket flask. There were rope tricks and clowns and barrel races and bronc bustin' but the thing everybody came for, the thing everybody wanted to see, was the bull ridin'.

Beat

You could get up close in those days. I stood right there by the gate, my eyes as big as saucers, as they led the biggest, ugliest, meanest looking bull I had ever seen in my life into the chute. Then this good old boy, more balls than brains, carefully climbed on board. He shoved his one gloved hand under the rope around the bull and worked it this way and that, checkin' his grip 'till he got it just right. The bull snorted once and every muscle on his body twitched. The good old boy took a breath. Nodded at his friends and said, "Here we go." They released the gate and twenty-seven hundred pounds of horns, hooves, and hate EXPLODED into the arena, twistin' left and right, buckin' up and down.

Beat

Everybody gets thrown. Everybody. Sometimes you come down so hard, you break your back. Sometimes the bull comes back and gores you and stomps you while you're lying there until they drive it away. Sometimes you don't ever get up. Why would you do that? Why would anybody do that? Well there was one moment in his short ride when I could see that good ole boy's face and maybe it was a trick of the light but there was such a look of joy. Of triumph.

Beat

Check your grip. Take a breath. *Here we go.*

LIGHTS SHIFT. CONGRESS. As LBJ moves to the podium, each Witness he passes addresses him:

WITNESSES   Mr. President. Mr. President. Mr. President.

TALLY BOARD(TB) reads: **JANUARY 4, 1965. STATE OF THE UNION ADDRESS. VIETNAM: 435 AMERICAN DEAD. 1,278 WOUNDED**

LBJ (*to Congress*)   The Great Society rests on abundance and liberty for all! It demands an end to poverty and racial injustice. We need a program to ensure every American child a quality education. We need a national health insurance plan for our seniors. We need a national effort to improve our inner cities, and we need the elimination of every remaining obstacle *to the right and the opportunity to VOTE!*

CONGRESS applauds. LIGHTS SHIFT. OVAL OFFICE *with* **VICE PRESIDENT HUMPHREY** *and* **SENATOR EVERETT DIRKSEN**, *Senate Minority Leader. LBJ has three TV sets going at all times (one for each network), a ticker-tape machine for immediate news releases, and several National newspapers, all of which he consults constantly.*

SENATOR EVERETT DIRKSEN   One hundred and four bills!?

TB: **List of all the Bills proposed.**

LBJ   Everett, I don't want to start out fightin', 'cause I'm not runnin' for re-election here ...

SENATOR EVERETT DIRKSEN   ... No, you're running for Santa Claus! Medicare. Education. Poverty programs ...

LBJ   . . . We're a great country but we can be better. And we can't do it without Senator Everett Dirksen.

SENATOR EVERETT DIRKSEN   And the butcher's bill?

LBJ   We're sittin' on the greatest economic expansion in the history of the Republic!

VICE PRESIDENT HUBERT HUMPHREY   The money is there.

SENATOR EVERETT DIRKSEN   This is not just a Republican issue; the Chairman of the Ways and Means Committee is also unhappy about the cost.

LBJ   When was the last time you saw Wilbur Mills happy about anything? Man was born with a lemon in his mouth.

SENATOR EVERETT DIRKSEN   Do not come to me for a tax increase.

LBJ   There's plenty of fat in the budget and I'm goin' after it with a tomahawk! Hell, we got military bases we haven't used since World War I.

SENATOR EVERETT DIRKSEN *(slightly worried)*   None in Illinois, I trust.

LBJ *(vaguely threatening)*   Still in the process of sortin' that out.

SENATOR EVERETT DIRKSEN   Even if you magically find the money, these new programs of yours are rife with burdensome regulations.

VICE PRESIDENT HUMPHREY *(skeptically)*   "Minority hiring policies?"

SENATOR EVERETT DIRKSEN   Why is the Federal Government always the solution? At the very least, if you're gonna insist on your little "social experiments" they should be managed by *local government*.

   LBJ glances at Humphrey.

LBJ   Sometimes local government is the problem.

VICE PRESIDENT HUMPHREY   Certainly that's true in Selma, Alabama.

LBJ   You read Governor Wallace's latest?

LBJ hands Dirksen a newspaper. SPOT on Wallace in Witness Box.

GOVERNOR WALLACE   These demonstrators in Selma, many of whom have been cited by the Justice Department as subversives, are part of this left-wing monster which sets "Civil Rights" as supreme to all! In reality, it's a conspiracy to destroy our freedom and our liberty!

SPOT out on Wallace.

LBJ *(drily)*   They're demonstrating for Voting Rights.

SENATOR EVERETT DIRKSEN   Look, I certainly don't carry water for Wallace but this breakneck pace of agitation by Dr. King is not reform, it's revolution, and revolutions have a way of devouring their own.

VICE PRESIDENT HUMPHREY   These new programs are simply tied to the standards set in the '64 Civil Rights Bill.

LBJ   A bill you made possible.

SENATOR EVERETT DIRKSEN   Passing a Bill is one thing; *funding* it is another. It's not just Mills; *many* Democrats share my concerns.

LBJ   South of the Mason Dixon line?

SENATOR EVERETT DIRKSEN   You still have Democrats there? Aside from Wallace, I mean.

LBJ   If I were you, I'd be less worried about what the South needs and more concerned about what Chicago wants. Mayor Daley is *extremely* interested in these bills and the Federal funding that comes with them but maybe I should just let you and Dick work that out.

LBJ's Secretary, **SALLY CHILDRESS** *runs in.*

SALLY CHILDRESS   Doctor King is here. And Senator Kennedy is on Line One.

SENATOR EVERETT DIRKSEN   Your election victory was impressive, Mr. President. The problem comes when you begin to act as if your mandate was from God and not the American people.

LBJ   We're gonna make history here, Everett. Join us and a hundred years from now school children will only know two names, Abraham Lincoln and—Everett Dirksen!

Dirksen laughs and leaves. LBJ presses Speaker Phone but signals Humphrey to remain quiet. SPOT on **SENATOR BOBBY KENNEDY** *and his aide,* **ADAM WALINSKY**. *Bobby indicates to Walinsky that he, too, should remain a silent listener.*

LBJ (*CONT'D*)   *Senator* Kennedy!

SENATOR BOBBY KENNEDY   Mr. President, congratulations again on your victory!

LBJ mimes masturbatory gesture to Humphrey re Senator Bobby Kennedy.

LBJ   It's not a victory of party or person, it's a tribute to the program that was begun by your brother *and it's a mandate for Unity.* Our nation needs to forget petty differences and stand united before the world. We gotta lot of work to do!

SENATOR BOBBY KENNEDY   You know you can count on my support.

LBJ   I know I can.

LBJ hangs up; turns to Humphrey. Kennedy turns to Walinsky.

LBJ You hear that? Not a fucking word of thank you! He never would have won New York without my help.	**SENATOR BOBBY KENNEDY** You hear that, Adam? "A mandate for Unity." That means "My way or the highway!"
VICE PRESIDENT HUMPHREY (*diplomatically*) I think it was implicit in what he said.	**ADAM WALINSKY** You think that tiger was gonna change his stripes?

13

LBJ   Treacherous little shit.

SENATOR BOBBY KENNEDY   Backstabbing son of a bitch.

LBJ   *Loyalty is everything,* Hubert.

SENATOR BOBBY KENNEDY   Never had an ounce of loyalty in him.

LIGHTS OUT on Kennedy / Walinsky

LBJ (*CONT'D*)   Any Committee openings, I want Johnson men who will kiss my ass in Macy's window and say it smells like roses. And tell all the Chairmen I want them to get their hearings goin' right NOW! Medicare is Number One! I'll go a hundred million or a billion on health. I'll spend the goddamn money.

VICE PRESIDENT HUMPHREY   The AMA is putting up a very stiff fight.

LBJ   I'll deal with those sons of bitches. Education?

VICE PRESIDENT HUMPHREY   Powell can't get it out of committee.

LBJ   He can, he just won't. (*Yelling to Sally*) Sally, get me Adam Clayton Powell on the phone! And send in Dr. King! (*back to Humphrey*) Powell's got his panties in a twist over some bullshit staffing supplement. That man is more crooked than a dog's hind leg.

   MLK enters. LBJ shakes his hand warmly.

LBJ (*CONT'D*)   Dr. King. Good to see you.

MLK   And you, Mr. President. I came as soon as I could but our Voting Rights campaign in Selma has reached a critical point.

LBJ   That's exactly what I want to talk to you about . . .

   Sally steps in.

SALLY CHILDRESS   . . . Representative Powell on Line One!

LBJ (*to MLK*)   Excuse me a moment . . .

14

Sally exits. LBJ stabs the button and picks up the phone. LIGHT on **ADAM CLAYTON POWELL** *in Bimini. An attractive* **WAITRESS** *brings him a drink as a steel band plays.*

LBJ $(CONT'D)$ Adam ...

ADAM CLAYTON POWELL ... Mr. President! How nice to ...

LBJ ... why the hell you blackmailin' me?!

ADAM CLAYTON POWELL No, no, that's not true, Mr. President.

LBJ Apparently 400,000 dollars to hire some short-skirted secretaries is more important to you than passin' 1.2 *billion* for school kids. You damn near single-handedly defeated the best Education bill the country has ever seen. You proud of yourself?

ADAM CLAYTON POWELL Now, Mr. President, I been loyal from way back, don't you think I'm entitled to that money?

LBJ You're not entitled to a goddamn thing! You looked me straight in the eye and said, "I'll get this Bill on the floor ..."

ADAM CLAYTON POWELL ... by March first!

LBJ Hell no, you said you were gonna *do it right away*, and then you ran off and they're killin' me! Thirty-two amendments while you're sippin' cocktails and chasin' pussy in Bimini! You get your ass back to Washington and report that Bill out *now*, no ifs, ands, or buts, and don't talk to me about no goddamn personal appropriations!

LBJ hangs up. LIGHTS OUT on Powell. LBJ turns back to MLK.

LBJ $(CONT'D)$ Selma.

MLK You know how they do things down there. When I was in jail last week, there were more Negroes with me in prison than there are on the Voting rolls. They keep us out with Literacy Tests, Character Referrals, the Poll Tax ...

VICE PRESIDENT HUBERT HUMPHREY ... the usual squalid voter suppression tactics ...

LBJ   . . . which the Justice department is aggressively challenging.

MLK   A case at a time? It'll take another hundred years. In the meantime . . .

Sally steps back in.

SALLY CHILDRESS   . . . Mr. Ackley of the Economic Council is here to see you.

LBJ   Reschedule.

SALLY CHILDRESS   We have once already . . .

LBJ   . . . Well, Sally, then I guess we'll do it again, won't we?

Sally leaves.

MLK   In the meantime, Sheriff Clark and the local authorities are just *brutalizing* our people. Somebody is going to get seriously injured, or worse; things are reaching a *crisis*.

A moment. This is news to LBJ.

LBJ   The last thing you want is a race riot.

MLK   Of course. That's why . . .

LBJ   . . . 'Cause that will play right into Governor Wallace's hands . . .

MLK   . . . *that's why we need Federal intervention.*

Sally runs back in; waves at LBJ.

LBJ   That is just not going to happen, Dr. King.

MLK   Why not?

LBJ   We can certainly get the FBI to keep tabs on the situation . . .

MLK   The FBI.

LBJ   *(to Sally)*   What?

SALLY CHILDRESS   Robert McNamara, sir. Says it's urgent.

LBJ Two minutes. (*to King*) Look, we are very close to gettin' my Poverty programs passed . . .

MLK . . . And we're all excited at the prospect but Selma . . .

LBJ (*confidingly*) . . . For obvious reasons I'm not publicizing how much of this eight billion dollars is goin' to Negroes but most of these programs are geared to people makin' under $2,000 a year and I think we both know who we're talkin' about but *this business in Selma could jeopardize all of that.*

VICE PRESIDENT HUMPHREY The swing votes in Congress are once again the Southern Democrats. The prospect of all that Federal funding might get them on board but . . .

LBJ . . . .not if we push them too hard on Voting Rights.

MLK We are in Selma because *you* encouraged us to bring attention to the problems of voting in the South! "We're in this together," you said. And then you told me to find the "worst condition" out there and get it on the radio and the TV until even that fellow sitting on a tractor would say, "Well, that's just not fair."

LBJ We don't disagree on tactics, Dr. King, just on *timing*. We're still in this together.

MLK Are we? When do you actually submit a Voting Rights Bill to Congress?

LBJ Soon. But for now, I need you to pull in your horns down there in Selma until I get these programs passed.

MLK Let me understand, despite your promise, you are not prepared to even offer a Voting Rights Bill . . .

LBJ . . . right now . . .

MLK . . . or provide us any meaningful protection while we demonstrate against policies which you yourself deplore, while simultaneously making us responsible for any violence that local authorities unleash on our non-violent demonstrators.

LBJ Keep the pressure on, highlight the issues, but don't give them any excuse.

A moment. MLK regard LBJ with more sadness then anger.

MLK This is the South, Mr. President; they don't need any excuse to beat Negroes.

MLK leaves. LBJ glances at Humprey.

LBJ Don't give me that look. I had the Attorney General start drafting a Voting Rights Bill a month ago. *(punches phone button)* Get me Hoover!

VICE PRESIDENT HUMPHREY Why not share that with Dr. King?

LBJ Because I don't know what I'm going to do, or when I'm gonna do it, but I damn sure like to keep my options open. We're only gonna get one shot at this in Congress and they're not ready yet. *(On phone)* Jay!

*SPOT on **J. EDGAR HOOVER** up. His aide, **DEKE DELOACH**, stands nearby.*

J. EDGAR HOOVER *(on phone)* Mr. President?

LBJ You're supposed to be on top of things in Selma! Why do I have Dr. King in here tellin' me it's going to hell in a handbasket before the FBI does?

J. EDGAR HOOVER I'm sure King has his own reasons for exaggerating the situation. Did he ask for Federal intervention? Our informants in both the Klan and the Sheriff's department report no unusual activities despite the considerable provocation of King and company.

LBJ I do not want to be blind-sided, Jay. *You keep a very close eye on things.* You understand?

J. EDGAR HOOVER *(on phone)* Yes, sir.

LBJ hangs up.

DEKE DELOACH   Increase our surveillance?

LBJ   The most important thing right now are my domestic programs. I don't want *anything* to get in the way of that.

J. EDGAR HOOVER (*nodding*)   But under no circumstances are agents to intervene on behalf of the protesters.

SPOT OUT on Hoover/Deloach.

MCNAMARA *enters and hands LBJ a cable.*

ROBERT MCNAMARA   Mr. President, we have a situation in Saigon—President Khanh has suffered some kind of nervous breakdown and the Generals are plotting another coup. The whole government could collapse.

LBJ (*shaking his head*)   Ever since Kennedy had Diem assassinated, it's been a revolving door over there.

ROBERT MCNAMARA   Ambassador Taylor thinks he can keep the Vietnamese Generals calm for now but the Joint Chiefs believe we should immediately apply maximum military pressure to bolster the South's defenses.

VICE PRESIDENT HUMPHREY (*incredulous*)   They want to go to war?

LBJ   They always want to go to war. I need another option, Bob. Vietnam will eat up everything I'm trying to do domestically.

ROBERT MCNAMARA   I disagree with the Chiefs. I think the North Vietnamese are no different than we are and will adapt their behavior to a political calculus of cost and benefit.
   If we *gradually* increase military pressure they will eventually recognize the futility of hostilities and we'll be able to *negotiate* our way out.

LBJ   Crawl up Uncle Ho's pant's leg an inch at a time until he unloads his pistol?

ROBERT MCNAMARA   But start with a show of force. Immediate deployment of two groups of fixed wing aircraft to a new base to be constructed at Pleiku in the Central Highlands . . .

LBJ   . . . a *land* base?

VICE PRESIDENT HUMPHREY   Our first land base in Vietnam?

ROBERT MCNAMARA   Technically, that is correct.

VICE PRESIDENT HUMPHREY   It's either correct or it's not correct.

ROBERT MCNAMARA   It's rarely that simple, Mr. Vice President.

VICE PRESIDENT HUMPHREY   And that land base means with all the usual security personnel . . . ?

ROBERT MCNAMARA   . . . That goes without saying . . .

LBJ   . . . but no active *ground troops*. No army. No Marines.

ROBERT MCNAMARA (*nodding*)   That's right. And then we can substantially increase our air strikes as the need arises.

A moment.

LBJ   Christ, I feel like a catfish that's bit a big juicy worm only to find a right sharp hook in the middle of it.

VICE PRESIDENT HUMPHREY   Mr. President, by increasing the bombing and adding troops . . .

ROBERT MCNAMARA   . . . We're not adding troops . . . !

VICE PRESIDENT HUMPHREY   . . . maintenance and security . . .

LBJ   . . . *Those aren't troops!* You heard Bob, we're not adding troops!

VICE PRESIDENT HUMPHREY   Alright but it seems to me that this will take you in Goldwater's direction. Why? We stressed not enlarging the war and won by a landslide.

LBJ   What are you advocating?

VICE PRESIDENT HUMPHREY   I think we should cut our losses *now*.

ROBERT MCNAMARA Withdraw? The Vietnamese Government will collapse and Ho Chi Minh will be having breakfast in Saigon the next day.

LBJ I am not going to be the American President who lost Asia!

ROBERT MCNAMARA That's the beauty of the graduated system. We increase the pressure just enough to drive them to the negotiating table without alarming China or the Soviet Union.

LBJ Or Congress. I want their focus on my domestic programs.

  Beat

Alright, planes on the ground and we'll increase the air strikes but *I choose the targets.*

ROBERT MCNAMARA The Pentagon will want to retain control . . .

LBJ . . . I'm the Commander in Chief and I'll damn well choose!

ROBERT MCNAMARA Yes, sir.

LBJ How are those base closures coming?

ROBERT MCNAMARA I estimate the cost savings at something like a billion dollars or more.

LBJ Wilbur Mills will shit himself! How many of those bases are in Illinois?

ROBERT MCNAMARA Illinois? I don't know exactly but I'll get back to you right away.

LBJ Illinois is critical in a lot of ways. And Robert? Keep a tight lid on this new airbase. There's no value in letting the Press know, they'll just blow it up. You understand?

ROBERT MCNAMARA I don't think it requires any announcement on our part.

  McNamara leaves.

VICE PRESIDENT HUMPHREY The press will find out sooner or later.

LBJ At which point we'll deal with it! (*a challenge*) I need to be able to trust you on this, Hubert. You understand? You're my point man on the Great Society. I never had any influence when I was vice president 'cause Kennedy wouldn't give me none but I'm not going to do you that way. It's gonna be Johnson and Humphrey, half and half, so let's get going!

LBJ gestures and Humphrey leaves. SPOT on LBJ.

LBJ (*to Audience*) "Oh my God, he's lying!" Like that never happened before in the history of the Republic. George Washington and his fucking cherry tree.

Beat

What I know is this. As a kid in the Hill Country all the women I grew up with, my mother and my grandmother and my aunts, they were beat down and broke 'fore the age of thirty by a miserable dog's life, draggin' buckets of water every day back to the house, or wandering for miles, gathering fire wood for heatin' and cookin' and washin' and cleanin'. Their backs were bent and their hands were crabbed and all their beauty and promise was stolen from them. So when I went to Washington for the first time I did whatever I had to do to bring electricity to my part of the world. I begged, I pleaded, I kissed up, I bent over, and yeah, I told a lie or two. But when that first electric bulb went in and chased the bleak darkness of the Texas night away or when that first electric pump brought water into the house at the turn of a tap, do you think any of those women thought, "Oh no, I can't use this, *Lyndon lied.*"

Beat

You wanta plow a straight furrow, you put blinders on your mule so he don't get startled and run off. Politics, it ain't no different.

*SPOT out on LBJ. SPOT up on HOTEL ROOM, SELMA, ALABAMA. MLK with **RALPH ABERNATHY**, **BOB MOSES**, and **STOKELY CARMICHAEL**.*

*TB reads: **SELMA, ALABAMA. FEBRUARY, 1965. VIETNAM: 489 AMERICAN DEAD. 1,448 WOUNDED.***

BOB MOSES   The man is a liar! The surprise is not that LBJ reneged on his promise to submit a Voting Rights Bill; the surprise is that you believed him in the first place.

MLK looks exhausted; worn out.

MLK   The Bill is not dead, Bob . . .

STOKELY CARMICHAEL   . . . but it is beginnin' to stink a little.

RALPH ABERNATHY   His Poverty Programs, Stokely, will be an enormous help to our people.

STOKELY CARMICHAEL   If they pass!

BOB MOSES   *Voting Rights.*

MLK   He doesn't oppose the Selma campaign.

BOB MOSES   But he won't publicly *support* it, will he?

MLK   Not right now.

BOB MOSES   Will he at least send in Federal protection?

MLK   The FBI.

The Men all look at one another and laugh.

RALPH ABERNATHY   Well. Now I feel safe.

More laughter.

BOB MOSES   Not even Federal Marshals? It's Freedom Summer all over again. *Somebody is gonna die.*

MLK   Are we registering anybody?

BOB MOSES   The game hasn't changed. Every day we get a hundred volunteers or more to stand outside the Courthouse, rain or shine, and wait to see the Registrar—risking their jobs, their homes, and their lives.

STOKELY CARMICHAEL And every day, Sheriff Clark does everything he can to keep'em out.

BOB MOSES Last four weeks we got a grand total of fifty-seven people inside to finally see the Registrar ...

STOKELY CARMICHAEL ...And all of 'em were "disqualified."

RALPH ABERNATHY (*delicately*) And the press is losing interest.

MLK (*shaking his head*) How discouraged are people?

STOKELY CARMICHAEL They aren't discouraged; they're *mad*. This morning, Annie Lee Cooper took a swing at Sheriff Clark; shook that cracker up. His eyes got big as that fucking "NO" button he wears on his helmet. I thought for a moment he was gonna blow a gasket! (*laughter*) Then three deputies held Annie Lee down while Clark beat her with his nightstick. Our young men see much more of that and we won't be able to hold'em back. Maybe we shouldn't.

BOB MOSES Stokely.

STOKELY CARMICHAEL What? We can't talk about this?

MLK About what?

STOKELY CARMICHAEL Maybe non-violence doesn't work anymore.

MLK (*sharply*) There is no other way.

Stokely shrugs, not inclined to have it out now.

MLK Announce a Night March.

BOB MOSES Martin.

MLK Not in Selma; nearby.

STOKELY CARMICHAEL (*nodding approval*) Marion is thirty miles away ...

RALPH ABERNATHY ...and outside Sheriff Clark's jurisdiction.

BOB MOSES   It's still dangerous.

MLK   What do you want, Bob? You tell me it's not working, so what else can we do? We have to up the stakes. We've got to make people aware . . .

MLK suddenly staggers, then sits down heavily. Everyone crowds around. MLK shakes his head.

MLK (*CONT'D*)   I'm OK! I'm OK. Just need to rest for a minute.

LIGHTS SHIFT. EVERYONE leaves MLK alone. COMPANY members become **CONGREGATES** *and begin singing a slow Civil Rights hymn. MLK is joined by a young, soft-spoken black man,* **JIMMY LEE JACKSON.**

JIMMY LEE JACKSON   My name is Jimmy Lee Jackson and I'm twenty-six years old. I earn six dollars a day as a pulpwood cutter in Marion, Alabama. I'm the youngest deacon at St. James Baptist Church and I have tried to register to vote five times. I wasn't even at the night march. After it got dark, four hundred protesters—men, women and kids—left the church in Marion and were on their way to the courthouse when they was stopped in the square by a buncha police and Sheriff Clark from Selma. Don't know why Clark was there—just wanted in on the fun, I guess.

SPOT on **SHERIFF CLARK**. *He stands up in the gallery with a bullhorn.*

SHERIFF CLARK   NOW ALL YOU PEOPLE NEED TO DISPERSE, OR RETURN TO YOUR CHURCH!

JIMMY LEE JACKSON   Nobody was resistin' or nothin'; Reverend Dobynes was very respectful.

REVEREND DOBYNES *stands up in the gallery.*

REVEREND DOBYNES   I'd like to pray for a moment, if I could?

JIMMY LEE JACKSON   Then the street lights all went out.

Overhead, the STAGE LIGHTS flicker; then SHIFT to an acute angle, throwing shadows across the STAGE.

And it was dark as the bottom of a well. Two deputies clubbed Reverend Dobynes and dragged him off and then the rest of them waded into the crowd.

The WITNESSES begin pounding on the gallery walls. There are SOUNDS of SCREAMS and SCUFFLING. Fragmented B&W IMAGES on the TB reads: **POLICEMAN swinging a club; broken glass; WOMAN cowering; blood on the sidewalk. Etc.**

The policemen chased people back to the church and all the way into the town, clubbin' everybody they saw. My eighty-two year old granddaddy, Cager Lee, wasn't doin' nothin' but he got caught up in the mess and tried to duck into Mack's Cafe to get away. Ten State Troopers followed him, smashin' lights, breakin' dishes, and beatin' anybody they could find. When they started beatin' on Cager, my momma, Viola, tried to pull 'em off her daddy but they beat her to the floor. I tried to protect my momma but a State Trooper threw me 'gainst the cigarette machine while another one shot me two times in the stomach, and then they both drove me outside, beatin' me the whole time like a dog, until I collapsed.

Violent "BEATING" of set morphs into a quiet rhythmic pulse, like a HEARTBEAT.

In the distance, the SOUND of an approaching ambulance siren.

They kept the ambulance away for three hours 'fore they finally allowed people to get me to Good Samaritan Hospital. While I lay there, Sheriff Clark served me with a warrant for disturbing the peace.

SIREN stops. **CORETTA** *enters the light. She doesn't "see" Jimmy.*

On Friday, February 26, at 8:10 in the morning, I died.

HEARTBEAT stops.

My name is Jimmy Lee Jackson. I was the youngest deacon at St. James Baptist Church. I tried to register to vote five times.

Company members quietly begin to sing a mournful hymn.

MLK (*to Coretta*)   I shoulda been there.

CORETTA   Thank God you weren't. That young man's death wasn't your fault.

Jimmy Lee walks off. MLK watches him go.

MLK   Whose was it?

CORETTA   The white cops who shot him and then wouldn't let him see a doctor while he bled to death!

MLK   Marion was my idea.

Coretta hugs him.

CORETTA   No more marches?

A moment. Hymn stops.

MLK   One more.

LIGHTS SHIFT. OVAL OFFICE. LBJ, MLK and Humphrey.

LBJ (*incredulous*)   *You are outta your mind!*

MLK   I asked you for Federal protection.

LBJ   Don't you dare put that boy's death on me!

MLK   So we will now hold a memorial march for Jimmy Lee Jackson from Selma, Alabama to the state capital, Montgomery, and present our demands for the right to vote directly to Governor Wallace. Like Moses, we will confront Pharaoh to his face.

VICE PRESIDENT HUMPHREY   Eighty miles along the Jefferson Davis Highway through the worst Klan country in the South.

LBJ   You are gonna get people killed!

MLK   Our people are already being killed!

LBJ   Then why are you throwing more gas on the fire? You ought to be calming folks down.

MLK   That is exactly what I am doing. This march will take several days of hard physical work that will transform their anger into a clear focus on what matters—*the right to vote.* Which if we had—if you had kept your promise—none of this would have happened.

LBJ   How do you think this works, Doctor—I just tell Congress what to do and they do it?! You know damn well Governor Wallace is not gonna protect you.

MLK   What happens to me is unimportant.

LBJ   What happens to this country is not! Another death and all hell will break loose.

MLK   That is why we hope the Federal Government will provide the marchers with protection. *This time.*

LBJ   You think you can twist my arm like this? You are putting everything we have and everything we hope for in jeopardy and whatever happens is on your head! *You are on your own.*

Sally enters quickly.

SALLY CHILDRESS   Secretary McNamara and General Westmoreland, sir.

MLK (*coldly*)   Certainly, Mr. President, you will have to act as your conscience guides you but with you or without you, *we will march.*

MLK leaves with Sally as McNamara and **GENERAL WESTMORELAND** *enter.*

ROBERT MCNAMARA (*pained*)   Mr. President, early this morning Viet Cong attacked our base in Pleiku. Eight American servicemen were killed, a hundred wounded, and more than twenty aircraft were destroyed.

LBJ (*quietly*)   Our boys gettin' everything they need?

GENERAL WESTMORELAND   We're flying the wounded to an army hospital in Germany.

LBJ   And our "allies?"

ROBERT MCNAMARA   Unfortunately, President Khanh was arrested by units of the South Vietnamese army an hour ago.

LBJ   So, who's running the damn country?

ROBERT MCNAMARA   Effectively, I suppose, we are, at least temporarily. The Chiefs strongly recommend a retaliatory air strike against the North Vietnamese as the *beginning* of a more open-ended air campaign . . .

GENERAL WESTMORELAND   . . . Operation Rolling Thunder. Round the clock carpet bombing of infiltration routes and military installations.

VICE PRESIDENT HUMPHREY   Jesus.

GENERAL WESTMORELAND   And send in two battalions of Marines to guard Pleiku.

LBJ   How many men is that?

GENERAL WESTMORELAND   Thirty-five hundred men.

A moment.

LBJ   Ground troops.

GENERAL WESTMORELAND   For security purposes, yes.

LBJ   Well, that's closing the barn door after the horse is out?! There's no other alternative?

GENERAL WESTMORELAND   We have to protect our men and we obviously cannot rely on our South Vietnamese allies.

LBJ   Thank you, General.

General Westmoreland exits.

Marines. You know how this is gonna look?

ROBERT MCNAMARA   We only have two choices: expand military action against the North to increase pressure for a settlement, or withdraw and face an increase in Communist power worldwide.

A moment.

LBJ   Maybe we could call those Marines, "Military Police?"

ROBERT MCNAMARA   Marines aren't MP's and everybody knows that but I guess we could call them, "Security Battalions."

LBJ   All right. My answer is yes but my judgement is no.

ROBERT MCNAMARA   I'm cold as hell on this myself but I don't see any other solution. We'll announce late so it won't make the morning edition. There will be headlines, of course . . .

LBJ emits a quiet loony laugh.

LBJ   You think there's a chance of that, do ya?

LBJ gestures and McNamara leaves.

VICE PRESIDENT HUBERT HUMPHREY   I think this escalation is going to be very confusing to the American people. All we have is a very thin claim of National Security.

LBJ   If I don't act, the Right-wingers will hammer me for being soft on communism. I don't need to worry about the Left.

VICE PRESIDENT HUBERT HUMPHREY   I disagree . . .

Sally enters.

SALLY CHILDRESS   Bobby Kennedy is here. And also President Appel of the American Medical Association with several board members.

LBJ   One minute, Sally. (*to Humphrey*) The AMA still screwing us on Medicare?

VICE PRESIDENT HUBERT HUMPHREY   They've proposed their own Bill, "Elder Care"—a voluntary program, available only if each individual state signs up.

LBJ   That's not, "Elder Care," that's, "I don't care." Sally, send Bobby in. And tell the press to get ready for a major announcement.

SALLY CHILDRESS   What announcement?

LBJ   The one I'm gonna make in about ten minutes!

Sally leaves.

Talk to Katzenbach and see if there's any way we can stop, or at least delay, King's march.

Humphrey leaves as Bobby enters.

SENATOR BOBBY KENNEDY   Mr. President . . .

LBJ (*coldly*)   Senator Kennedy, you are the only remainin' obstacle to my Education Bill. I expect to fight Dirksen but the liberal Senator from New York? Are you opposed to helpin' poor people acquire an education?

SENATOR BOBBY KENNEDY   Of course, not, Mr. President, I'm simply concerned that in this well-meaning but vaguely constructed bill we are just throwing money at the problem.

LBJ   I had my task force workin' on these issues for months; college professors, experts in the field; your kinda people.

SENATOR BOBBY KENNEDY   The intention is fine, it's the execution. If we pour all this money into school systems which are, in some cases, the source of the problem, aren't we just wasting our money?

LBJ   I wouldn't ordinarily have thought of you as so frugal, given your background and all.

SENATOR BOBBY KENNEDY (*bristling*)   I take my fiduciary responsibilities very seriously.

31

LBJ I'm sure you do but see, we're tryin' to get an Education Bill passed and I know a little somethin' about this 'cause of my background. Right out of college I needed to find me a job and of course, my daddy couldn't help me in that regard, and so I became a teacher. And let me tell you, Senator, nobody works harder than a teacher and they are naturally protective of their prerogatives, so in order to achieve buy-in with the local districts we had to give them control of the programs.

SENATOR BOBBY KENNEDY Was this to achieve their buy-in, or Senator Russell's?

LBJ If you have another pocketful of votes handy, Senator, feel free to pass them along.

SENATOR BOBBY KENNEDY The Bill feels under-developed; we are essentially being asked to pass now, and ask questions later.

LBJ I think of myself as a farmer sowin' seeds. I got to get my crop in the ground now, while the sun is shinin', and later there will be a time to cultivate and to reap.

SENATOR BOBBY KENNEDY But there are no standards at all!

LBJ Do you want an Education Bill in your lifetime or not?!

A moment.

SENATOR BOBBY KENNEDY What if we added an "evaluation" procedure to measure what difference we are making?

A moment.

LBJ I'll have my staff draft an amendment to that effect.

SENATOR BOBBY KENNEDY I'm happy to do that . . .

LBJ *. . . I'll take care of it.*

SENATOR BOBBY KENNEDY It's not the credit I'm after.

LBJ Then this shouldn't be a problem, should it?

LBJ turns his back to Kennedy and presses his phone.

Sally, you can send in those AMA folks now.

LBJ turns, "surprised" to find Kennedy still there.

Thank you for your help, Senator.

Bobby Kennedy exits as **PRESIDENT APPEL** *and other* **AMA MEMBERS** *enter.*

AMA PRESIDENT APPEL   Mr. President.

LBJ shakes hands and passes out souvenir pens.

LBJ   Dr. Appel. I appreciate you fellas stopping by on such short notice. Usually it's pretty hard to get a house call.

Polite laughter.

AMA PRESIDENT APPEL   Mr. President, our members are deeply concerned by this unprecedented intrusion by the Federal Government into the sacred relationship between doctor and patient.

LBJ   Who the hell's doing that?

AMA PRESIDENT APPEL   Your bill, sir. *Medicare.*

LBJ   Oh, I didn't bring you over here to talk about that stuff.

AMA PRESIDENT APPEL (*confused*)   You didn't?

LBJ   That mess is up to Congress; I gotta war to fight and the stakes couldn't be higher. If we lose Vietnam, what's next? Thailand? Indonesia? Australia? Our boys are fightin' hard but at the same time, we also need to be winnin' the hearts and minds of the Vietnamese people. Now, Gentlemen, we got the best damn doctors in the world and I been thinkin', what if some of your members volunteered to open up a coupla clinics over there, just for a few weeks at a time, to tend to those people? You save a man's son from lockjaw or get his wife safely through labor, he's gonna look at America a whole different way. Might make a huge difference to the safety of our young men.

Appel glances at the other members.

AMA PRESIDENT APPEL   Well, sure, Mr. President. I'm sure we can put together something along those lines.

LBJ   Would ya? By God that's great! Tell you what, let's share this good news with the press right now. (*shouting to secretary*) SALLY! YOU CAN BRING'EM IN NOW!

The PRESS surges in.

Ladies and Gentlemen of the Press, I am very pleased to announce an extraordinary act of generosity by the AMA! They are goin' to set up a system of volunteer health clinics all over Viet Nam to help ordinary Vietnamese people!

The PRESS is surprised but they dutifully applaud.

REPORTER#1   Mr. President! What about the Medicare Bill?

LBJ (*fierce*)   Now, you just hold on a second! I know you're tryin' to embarrass these good people but let me ask you something. Do you think for one second that the American Medical Association would give so generously in a patriotic gesture like this to help some Vietnamese peasant but refuse to help their own fella countrymen? Does that sound right to you?

LBJ puts his arm tightly around President Appel's shoulders.

Of course they're gonna support Medicare! Isn't that right, Dr. Appel?

Stunned, Appel looks at his fellow board members and then the press.

PRESIDENT APPEL   Sure.

CAMERAS flash. The stage empties. Sally enters.

SALLY CHILDRESS   Your appointment with Mr. Ackley, Council of Economic Advisors?

A moment.

LBJ Reschedule.

SALLY CHILDRESS Again?

LBJ Again. What?

Sally lays some papers on his desk.

SALLY CHILDRESS This is the information you requested, sir. The names and home addresses of those killed in action this month.

A moment. LBJ glances at the pages but doesn't pick them up. Sally starts to leave.

LBJ Your son write you regular?

Sally stops; surprised.

SALLY CHILDRESS Yes, sir. He's a good boy that way.

A moment.

LBJ USS Forestal, right? (*She nods*) The Navy treatin' him well? Feedin' him right?

SALLY CHILDRESS No complaints, sir.

A moment.

LBJ You tell him he's in my prayers.

SALLY CHILDRESS Yes, sir.

LBJ nods. Sally leaves. LBJ stares at the papers for a moment. He picks one up; glances at it.

LBJ Sergeant Richard B. Thompson.

LBJ presses his Dictaphone button.

"Dear Mr. and Mrs. Thompson. It is with a heavy heart I write to you regarding the loss of your son."

A moment.

"The tragic loss of your son."

A moment.

"The tragic loss of your brave son."

LBJ puts the paper down; the exhaustion seeping through. **LADY BIRD** *enters carrying a cupcake with a burning candle on it.*

LADY BIRD   Lyndon?

LBJ (*re: the cupcake*)   Whose birthday did I forget this time?

Lady Bird puts the cupcake down in front of LBJ.

LADY BIRD   Nobody. A little bird told me that you had a very good day today and that your Medicare and Education bills are as good as passed and I thought we should celebrate. Make a wish.

LBJ blows out the candle.

LBJ   You actually gonna let me eat this?

LADY BIRD   It's a cupcake.

LBJ   My wish came true.

LBJ begins peeling the paper away.

LADY BIRD   And it's low calorie.

LBJ pushes the cupcake away. A moment.

LBJ   They want me to send in Marines.

LADY BIRD   You swore you'd never do that.

LBJ   I gotta protect the airfields.

LADY BIRD   Is that what this is really about?

LBJ   What the Chiefs really want is for us to take over the war from the Vietnamese but I'll be damned if I'll do that 'cause we'll just wind up with the very people we're tryin' to save, bein' mad as hell at us. The great trouble I'm under is a man can fight if he's got—if he can see daylight down the road somewhere. I'm not sure there is any daylight in Vietnam, Bird.

Lady Bird hugs him. He accepts her embrace, then goes back to his papers.

I got to finish these.

LADY BIRD   You want a drink?

LBJ   I quit.

LADY BIRD *(startled)*   You did? Why?

LBJ   The Joint Chiefs; this mess in Selma with King. I need to keep a clear head.

LADY BIRD   Your eldest daughter is sweet on a boy.

LBJ   Lynda's too young.

LADY BIRD   She's just two years younger than I was when we got married. She wants you to meet him.

LBJ   I don't know.

LADY BIRD   Not right now. *(gently)* He's in the Marines.

SPOT OUT on LBJ/Lady Bird.

A female **SHERIFF'S AUXILIARY** *appears US wearing a large Button with a Confederate Flag on it and a Telephone Operator Headset.*

SHERIFF'S AUXILIARY   Can we have some quiet, please?! We're trying to monitor three radios!

Black Witnesses begin to sing "Walk With Me, Oh Lord" as they assemble.

TB reads: **PETTUS BRIDGE. SELMA, ALABAMA. SUNDAY, MARCH 7, 1965.**

LBJ moves SR where he will remain, monitoring the situation through phone hookup with Humphrey who is on the ground in SELMA.

SHERIFF'S AUXILIARY *(on radio)*   There's three more cars of niggers crossing the Pettus bridge and heading to their staging area at the

Brown Chapel in Selma. And some more white bastards riding with them. At least six hundred invaders or more.

SPOT on Governor Wallace (in Montgomery) and Alabama State Trooper, **COLONEL AL LINGO** *(in Selma) also talking on the phone.*

LBJ *(on phone)*   Where's King?

GOVERNOR WALLACE *(on phone)*   Where's King, Al?

HUMPHREY *(on phone)*   There was a bomb threat in Atlanta.

AL LINGO *(on phone)*   They cancelled his flight.

LBJ *(on phone)*   Jesus. Are they going ahead with the march anyway?

SPOT on BROWN CHAPEL. **JOHN LEWIS** *and* **HOSEA WILLIAMS** *are carefully taping newspapers to their legs beneath their trousers.*

VICE PRESIDENT HUMPHREY *(on phone)*   Looks like it. Two of his aides, John Lewis and Hosea Williams are running things in his place.

LBJ *(on phone)*   How about Wallace?

GOVERNOR WALLACE *(on phone)*   I don't want those niggers crossin' that Bridge, you hear me, Al? Not one of 'em.

COLONEL AL LINGO *(on phone)*   Yes, sir.

Lingo hangs up phone.

VICE PRESIDENT HUMPHREY *(on phone)*   Hiding out in Montgomery on "State Business."

SPOT out on Wallace.

COLONEL AL LINGO *(shouting off-stage)*   LET'S GO, FELLAS!

Lingo exits.

VICE PRESIDENT HUMPHREY *(on phone)*   But he's sent plenty of muscle to Selma. The only way to Montgomery is across the Pettus Bridge and there are two hundred State Troopers blocking it. Shotguns. Pistols. Tear gas. The works. In addition, there's Sheriff

Clark, his Deputies, and his own private army, the "Possemen." They're on horseback with whips, wooden clubs wrapped with barbed wire, and electric cattle prods.

McNamara enters Oval Office.

LBJ (*on phone*)   Jesus Christ, you'd think these boys were gonna fight Antietam all over again. Hold on.

LBJ covers the phone and talks to McNamara.

ROBERT MCNAMARA (*quietly*)   Both Marine Battalions have landed in Vietnam. There was no resistance whatsoever.

LBJ   Thank God for that. Keep me informed.

SHERIFF'S AUXILIARY (*on phone*)   Sheriff Clark? Colonel Lingo requests that you move your posse men *behind* his troopers. There's no tellin' what these animals might try so be ready for anything. And make sure all your people have their gas masks ready. Gettin' close now!

JAMES BEVEL (*wearing a yarmulke*) *runs in to* BROWN CHAPEL.

JAMES BEVEL   King wants us to postpone 'till he can get back.

HOSEA WILLIAMS   Not with that crowd out there; these people are *ready.*

JAMES BEVEL   What's with the newspapers?

JOHN LEWIS   Can't feel the cattle prods so much. What's with the beanie?

JAMES BEVEL   Police think twice about hitting you in the head.

HOSEA WILLIAMS   That really work, Bevel?

JAMES BEVEL   Probably as much as your newspapers.

Bevel helps himself to newspaper as a **YOUNG BLACK WOMAN** *hurries in.*

YOUNG BLACK WOMAN   The troopers have got tear gas! Ya'll know what to do?

HOSEA WILLIAMS   That shit'll blind you, man.

JOHN LEWIS   Just temporary. If you get hit, go to the side of the road and stand quietly. The important thing is not to panic; *don't give 'em any excuse to attack you.*

YOUNG BLACK WOMAN   Everybody signed their notification forms?

JAMES BEVEL   For what?

YOUNG BLACK WOMAN   Next of kin.

A moment.

JOHN LEWIS   Yeah, we good.

YOUNG BLACK WOMAN   Ya'll take care.

The Young Black Woman runs out.

JAMES BEVEL   Doc said if we did march, one of us was to stay behind as a backup in case of emergency.

JOHN LEWIS   Not me!   **HOSEA WILLIAMS**   I'm going!

JAMES BEVEL (*CONT'D*)   Man, you are some hard-ass Negroes. Flip for it?

Everybody pulls out a coin. They flip and compare. Bevel loses.

Shit! Two outta three?

Lewis and Williams laugh.

JOHN LEWIS   See ya on the other side, James.

JAMES BEVEL   Good luck.

William and Lewis "fall in" and begin marching in place, leading the other Marchers. Williams gestures to Lewis's backpack.

SHERIFF'S AUXILIARY (*on radio*)   OK! OK! The niggers are moving out now, approaching the bridge!

HOSEA WILLIAMS   What you got in that pack of yours, anyway? Kryptonite?

JOHN LEWIS   An apple, a toothbrush, and a book.

HOSEA WILLIAMS   Gonna do a little reading in jail?

JOHN LEWIS   Jail might be the best thing that could happen.

Colonel Al Lingo appears.

COLONEL AL LINGO   TROOPERS INTO POSITION!

*The **STATE TROOPERS** move quickly into a line between the Audience and the Marchers.*

SHERIFF'S AUXILIARY (*on radio*)   Here we go. (*under her breath as she continues to watch*) "Our Father who art in Heaven . . ."

JOHN LEWIS (*looking ahead*)   Jesus Christ.

SHERIFF'S AUXILIARY   . . . hallowed be Thy name.

LBJ (*on phone*)   Where are they now?

VICE PRESIDENT HUMPHREY (*on phone*)   Crossing the bridge.

SHERIFF'S AUXILIARY   "Thy Kingdom come, Thy will be done, on earth as it is in Heaven."

*TB: **IMAGES of the approach to Pettus Bridge and the Bridge itself.** The SOUND of WIND and restless HORSES grows. STAGE darkens. SPECIAL on Hosea and Lewis as they try to tamp down their increasing dread.*

HOSEA WILLIAMS   When I was in the Army in Germany, we captured bridges just like this.

JOHN LEWIS   You can have this one if you want.

SHERIFF'S AUXILIARY   "Give us this day, our daily bread."

JOHN LEWIS (*glancing over the side*)   How far down you think that water is?

41

HOSEA WILLIAMS   Hundred feet.

SHERIFF'S AUXILIARY   "Forgive us our trespasses . . . "

HOSEA WILLIAMS   Can you swim?

JOHN LEWIS   No.

HOSEA WILLIAMS   Me neither.

SHERIFF'S AUXILIARY   " . . . As we forgive those who trespass against us."

JOHN LEWIS   Well, I guess it don't much matter then, does it?

COLONEL AL LINGO   THAT'S FAR ENOUGH! THIS IS COLONEL AL LINGO OF THE ALABAMA STATE TROOPERS. IT WOULD BE DETRIMENTAL TO YOUR SAFETY TO CONTINUE THIS MARCH.

Hosea and Lewis stop.

SHERIFF'S AUXILIARY   "Lead us not into temptation."

LBJ (*on phone*)   What's goin' on?

VICE PRESIDENT HUMPHREY (*on phone*)   The troopers have stopped them.

SHERIFF'S AUXILIARY   "But deliver us from evil."

COLONEL AL LINGO   Troopers.

The Troopers strap on their Gas Mask—the rubber bug-eyed goggles give them a surreal, threatening quality—and then put on their helmets.

THIS IS AN UNLAWFUL ASSEMBLY! GO HOME OR GO TO YOUR CHURCH!

VICE PRESIDENT HUMPHREY   The troopers are putting on their gas masks. Everybody's on edge.

SHERIFF'S AUXILIARY   "For Thine is the Kingdom."

COLONEL AL LINGO   THIS MARCH WILL NOT CONTINUE. IS THAT CLEAR?

SHERIFF'S AUXILIARY   "And the Power."

HOSEA WILLIAMS   May we have a word with you, Colonel?

COLONEL AL LINGO   THERE IS NO WORD TO BE HAD.

SHERIFF'S AUXILIARY   "And the Glory."

Lingo glances at his men. The Troopers remove their nightsticks and begin a slow, cadenced beat with their batons.

COLONEL AL LINGO   YOU MUST LEAVE THIS AREA IMMEDIATELY. THIS IS YOUR FINAL WARNING.

SHERIFF'S AUXILIARY   "Forever and ever."

Terrified, Hosea and Lewis exchange looks but neither retreats.

COLONEL AL LINGO   TROOPERS—ADVANCE!

SHERIFF'S AUXILIARY   Amen.

COLONEL AL LINGO   GET THOSE GODDAMN NIGGERS!

SHERIFF'S AUXILIARY   AND GET THOSE GODDAMN WHITE NIGGERS, TOO!

As the Troopers rush forward and begin clubbing the Marchers, Lingo throws a tear gas cannister. Simultaneously, the Sheriff's Auxiliary, a plastic pitcher in her hands, slowly walks US until she stands behind Hosea and Lewis.

*TB: **explodes into actual footage** (Slow-Motion and distorted) **of "Bloody Sunday."***

Amplified and distorted SOUNDS of Horses on pavement as the Possemen charge. SOUNDS of Tear Gas shells exploding. FOG covers the stage. SOUNDS of: COUGHING and CHOKING; clubs BREAKING bones; SCREAMING; glass SMASHING; sirens; WAILING.

Lewis kneels. The Sheriff Auxiliary tips the pitcher and pours blood over his head. A STEAM WHISTLE cuts through the noise and everyone FREEZES. Lewis staggers to his feet, facing the audience.

JOHN LEWIS   I don't know how President Johnson can send troops to Vietnam but HE CAN'T SEND TROOPS TO SELMA, ALABAMA!

Stage empties. LIGHTS SHIFT. OVAL OFFICE. LBJ, Humphrey, and Hoover.

VICE PRESIDENT HUMPHREY   The press is calling it, "Bloody Sunday!" Basically, it was a police riot.

LBJ *(furious)*   Have we arrested the sons of bitches?

J. EDGAR HOOVER   We've made two arrests.

LBJ   *Two?!*

J. EDGAR HOOVER   Two of Clark's possemen. They assaulted an FBI agent.

LBJ   Was he trying to make an arrest?

J. EDGAR HOOVER   He was taking pictures.

LBJ   Let me understand. Fifty-seven men, women, and children were beaten, stomped, and sent to the hospital, and the only arrests are two guys who attacked an *FBI agent*—who was just standin' there, not actually doin' anythin' to stop this mess?!

J. EDGAR HOOVER   I realize, from a certain perspective, that doesn't look very good.

LBJ   No, Jay, it doesn't. Have you seen the television? *Ten thousand* people protestin' in Detroit led by Governor Romney. Guess the '68 campaign started early. Did you miss the 600 people outside the White House this morning wavin' signs and callin' me names? It's so bad even Dirksen is outraged.

J. EDGAR HOOVER   You didn't want Federal involvement.

LBJ You can't take a little initiative?! If one of your guys saw a bank robbery would I personally have to pick up a phone and tell 'em to do somethin'?

VICE PRESIDENT HUMPHREY King has called for volunteers *nationwide* and announced he will resume the march tomorrow . . .

LBJ *Tomorrow?!*

VICE PRESIDENT HUMPHREY Tomorrow, leading it himself this time. People are flying into Selma by the hundreds, including white ministers, nuns, and rabbis.

LBJ Any more good news?

VICE PRESIDENT HUMPHREY He has also asked the Federal Court to issue a restraining order forbidding Alabama from interfering with the march . . .

J. EDGAR HOOVER . . . and he wants you to . . .

J. EDGAR HOOVER Send in   **LBJ** Send in Federal Marshals!
Federal Marshals.

LBJ I can't do that; it'll look like I'm *advocatin'* the march and then that damn runt Wallace will blame me, claimin' the Federal government is "invadin' Alabama!" Of course, if I don't send in troops and there's a buncha killings, then Walter Cronkite and the rest of 'em blame me, sayin', "Mr. President, what did you do to prevent that violence?"

VICE PRESIDENT HUMPHREY The Attorney General has your Voting Rights Bill ready to go.

LBJ Not yet. Join King's petition as a Friend of the Court but *privately* see if we can't get the Judge to take his time and slow things down; let these people cool off.

LIGHTS SHIFT. MLK and Abernathy join LBJ, Humphrey, and Hoover.

MLK The Judge is now prohibiting the march while he "studies" the situation!

LBJ I'm surprised as you are . . .

MLK . . . Are you?

VICE PRESIDENT HUMPHREY It's frustrating but there's nothing any of us can do about it.

MLK He is suspending our constitutional rights!

LBJ Then he'll be overturned on appeal.

MLK It won't matter by then. Hundreds of people have flown in from all over the country to march *tomorrow morning*; momentum is on our side.

LBJ Even more reason to proceed carefully.

J. EDGAR HOOVER This is a *Federal* injunction. If you violate it, the Justice Department will jail you for contempt.

MLK You are condemning a man for being robbed!

J. EDGAR HOOVER You knew there was a possibility of violence!

RALPH ABERNATHY We're not the ones beatin' folks! You take up the issue of violence with Governor Wallace; they're the ones in the disgrace business!

MLK Ralph!

LBJ We're just askin' you to wait a few days.

VICE PRESIDENT HUMPHREY You'll have your march; you can trust the government on this.

MLK You say that, Mr. Vice President, but you have not been a Black Man in America for three hundred years. I cannot promise to obey this injunction.

MLK starts off.

LBJ   What if we could create some kind of *compromise*?

MLK stops.

MLK   Like what?

LBJ   An agreement. A secret agreement between you, Wallace, and the Federal Government. What if you marched across the bridge, Alabama authorities made their little stand for the cameras, and then you turned around?

MLK and Abernathy exchange looks.

MLK   I don't know.

VICE PRESIDENT HUMPHREY   No one would get hurt and you would've honored your promise to march but not violated the Federal injunction. You'd be praised for your restraint.

MLK   Negroes are not praised for restraint—we are expected to *be* restrained. I don't think you appreciate how angry people are. Next time demonstrators might shoot back!

LBJ   All the more reason to avoid this confrontation.

MLK   Even if I accepted your—secret agreement—I don't think you can get Wallace to keep his word even if we stop. Then we'd get blamed for marching AND for getting beat up.

Sound of Marchers singing "Ain't Nobody Gonna Turn Me Around."

LBJ   I'll deal with the Governor of Alabama.

LIGHTS SHIFT. INSIDE BROWN CHAPEL.

SPOT on MLK preaching to MARCHERS.

TB reads: **TUESDAY, MARCH 9, 1965. SELMA.**

MLK   I don't know what might happen today. They might attack us. They might jail us. But I tell you now, I would rather die marching for my rights, than live on my knees!

47

*LIGHTS SHIFT. OUTSIDE BROWN CHAPEL. Stokely
Carmichael works an overflow crowd of Marchers. Beside him are Moses
and Bevel.*

STOKELY CARMICHAEL   That is *your* bridge! You gotta right to
march across it! If Sheriff Jim Clark tries to stop you, what're you
gonna do?!

CROWD   March across it!

STOKELY CARMICHAEL   And if Colonel Al Lingo tries to stop you,
what're you gonna do?!

CROWD   March across it!

STOKELY CARMICHAEL   AND IF GOVERNOR GEORGE
WALLACE TRIES TO STOP YOU, WHAT'RE YOU GONNA
DO?!

CROWD   MARCH ACROSS IT!

STOKELY CARMICHAEL   AND IF THE FEDERAL
GOVERNMENT TRIES TO STOP YOU!?

CROWD   MARCH ACROSS IT!!

STOKELY CARMICHAEL   *AND IF MARTIN LUTHER KING
EVER COMES OUTTA THAT CHURCH AND TRIES TO
STOP YOU?!!*

CROWD   *MARCH ACROSS IT!!!*

LBJ in SPOT UR. Wallace in SPOT UL.

*LBJ is in phone contact with Humphrey and Wallace is in phone contact
with Colonel Al Lingo.*

LBJ (*on phone*)   How many marchers this time?

VICE PRESIDENT HUMPHREY (*on phone*)   Fifteen hundred people!

MLK and Abernathy join Stokely and others outside.

BOB MOSES (*to MLK*) You're really gonna do this, Doc? No turning around?

LBJ (*on phone*) King has agreed to the plan?

MLK All the way.

VICE PRESIDENT HUMPHREY (*on phone*) That is my understanding, yes.

MARCHERS FREEDOM NOW!

> *MLK/Abernathy/Stokely/Moses begin the march. SOUNDS of hundreds of others falling in step behind them.*

LBJ (*on phone*) And Wallace? He agreed to the plan?

MARCHERS FREEDOM NOW!

VICE PRESIDENT HUMPHREY (*on phone*) That's what he said.

GOVERNOR WALLACE (*on phone*) Where are they now, Al?

MARCHERS FREEDOM NOW!

> *TB:* **Ominous IMAGES of Pettus Bridge, filled with Troopers.**

COLONEL AL LINGO (*on phone*) The niggers are approachin' the bridge.

MARCHERS FREEDOM NOW!

COLONEL AL LINGO (*on phone*) The US Marshal is handin' King the Federal injunction and . . .

GOVERNOR WALLACE (*on phone*) . . . What's he doing? What's he doing!

COLONEL AL LINGO (*on phone*) King is wavin' the injunction aside as we all agreed.

> *Marchers applaud and cheer.*

GOVERNOR WALLACE (*on phone, gleeful*) So he's comin' on?

COLONEL AL LINGO (*on phone*)   Yes, sir. I'm gonna have to hang up now.

GOVERNOR WALLACE (*on phone*)   Al, you just do what I told you to do.

COLONEL AL LINGO (*on phone*)   You're sure about this, Governor?

GOVERNOR WALLACE (*on phone*)   *Just do it!*

Wallace hangs up. Lingo faces King and Abernathy as they approach.

COLONEL AL LINGO   Troopers!

Behind Lingo, a wall of Troopers forms up, blocking the way.

VICE PRESIDENT HUMPHREY (*on phone*)   Colonel Lingo is following the script, blocking the road. King is approaching him.

COLONEL AL LINGO   I am askin' you to stop where you are. We are here to see that this march will not continue.

MLK   We have a right to march to Montgomery.

COLONEL AL LINGO   You need to stop and turn around.

MLK glances back at his people.

MLK   May we have a moment to pray?

COLONEL AL LINGO   You can have your prayer, and then you must return to the church.

MLK kneels. His Group kneels with him; Abernathy right beside MLK.

LBJ (*on phone*)   What are they doin' now?

VICE PRESIDENT HUMPHREY (*on phone*)   King is praying. Everything is good so far.

LBJ (*on phone*)   How many troopers has Wallace got this time?

VICE PRESIDENT HUMPHREY (*on phone*)   Big show for the cameras. Five hundred State Troopers armed to the teeth.

MLK rises. Abernathy follows. SOUNDS of the Marchers rising.

OK, King is standing up now. Moment of truth.

GOVERNOR WALLACE (*to himself*)   *Now.*

COLONEL AL LINGO   TROOPERS! *MOVE TO THE SIDE OF THE HIGHWAY!*

The Troopers stand aside—the road to Montgomery is open. MLK is stunned; this is not the agreement.

VICE PRESIDENT HUMPHREY (*on phone*)   Holy shit!

LBJ (*on phone*)   What?! WHAT?!

VICE PRESIDENT HUMPHREY (*on phone*)   Wallace is pulling a fast one! The troopers have moved out of the way, clearing the road to Montgomery. Wallace is *trying to lure King into marching on.*

LBJ (*on phone*)   That backstabbing son of a bitch!

MLK glances at Abernathy who is as confused as he is.

RALPH ABERNATHY (*quietly*)   What the hell?

MLK considers the troopers.

MLK (*quietly to Abernathy*)   It's a trap. If we march any further, we're in violation of the Court Order and the troopers can attack us with impunity claiming we broke the law, and we all go to jail.

BOB MOSES (*calling out*)   What are you waiting for?!

MLK   If we don't march . . .

RALPH ABERNATHY   . . . Everybody will think you lost your nerve.

STOKELY CARMICHAEL   LET'S GO!

A moment. MLK makes his choice; the only choice he has.

MLK   WE WILL GO BACK TO THE CHURCH NOW!

MLK turns around and is quickly followed by Abernathy.

LBJ (*on phone*)   Jesus Christ, what's happenin'?!

BOB MOSES   Why are we turnin' around?!

STOKELY CARMICHAEL   What the fuck?! WHAT THE FUCK ARE WE DOIN'?!

VICE PRESIDENT HUMPHREY (*on phone*)   King is turning around!

COLONEL AL LINGO (*on phone*)   KING IS TURNING AROUND!

GOVERNOR WALLACE (*on phone, furious*)   WHAT?!

VICE PRESIDENT HUMPHREY (*on phone*)   He didn't fall into Wallace's trap!

COLONEL AL LINGO (*on phone*)   They're ALL turning around! All the marchers!

STOKELY CARMICHAEL   WHAT THE FUCK ARE WE DOIN'?!

Wallace hangs up, defeated.

GOVERNOR WALLACE   Goddamn.

LBJ (*furious*)   Get Governor Wallace up here. I think it's time somebody finally de-nutted that dog.

LIGHTS SHIFT to HOTEL, SELMA. Bob Moses is drinking by himself; is already wasted. MLK enters.

MLK   Where's Stokely?

BOB MOSES   Last I saw, curled up on the floor of his room, weeping. You broke more than your word out there today. Biggest show of national support the Movement has ever seen and then, at the critical moment, you turn around. Why was that?

MLK   I avoided a massacre that would have made Bloody Sunday look like a picnic.

BOB MOSES   *You betrayed us!*

MLK   I made a choice to protect people over preserving ideological purity.

52

BOB MOSES   Did you make a deal with the government?

MLK   I am continuing to negotiate with the Justice Department over this illegal injunction and . . .

BOB MOSES   . . . *Did you make a deal with the government at Pettus Bridge, yes or no?!*

MLK (*quietly*)   We are so very close to a Voting Rights Bill.

BOB MOSES   Even if they pass your goddamn Bill, they'll find a way. Remember how they fucked us over in Atlantic City?

MLK   I know.

BOB MOSES   You still believe in this "dream" of America. *I don't.* It's a lie. The motherfuckers are lying.

MLK (*very saddened*)   Please, Bob, don't quit on us; you're the best we've got.

Moses stands unsteadily.

BOB MOSES   I'm done, Doc. Done with you, done with the Movement, with all of it. And from now on, I will no longer speak to white people.

Moses walks off. LIGHTS shift. OVAL OFFICE. LBJ & Humphrey. Sally enters, followed by Governor Wallace and **SEYMORE TRAMMEL**.

SALLY CHILDRESS   Sir? It's Governor Wallace and his aide, Seymore Trammel.

GOVERNOR WALLACE   Mr. President. I appreciate the opportunity . . .

LBJ   . . . Have a seat, Governor.

LBJ physically steers Wallace to the smaller chair and pulls his own, larger chair, around until he is knee to knee with Wallace. LBJ ignores Trammel. Sally exits.

As you know, the Federal Judge has now rescinded his injunction and King is gonna have his march to Montgomery. So, you gonna keep those people safe?

SEYMORE TRAMMEL   The Governor is here to discuss the growin' menace of Communist demonstrations, not . . .

LBJ glares at Trammel like he was a dog who had just messed the carpet.

LBJ   Why don't you just sit there and take notes.

Trammel quickly sits down.

Now, I know you're not approvin' of brutality.

GOVERNOR WALLACE   There's no brutality in Alabama. In stoppin' that march we saved those peoples' lives.

LBJ picks up a folder off the coffee table and shuffles out a handful of 8 x 12 photographs.

LBJ   Really? Here's a few highlights shot by one of the FBI agents on Pettus Bridge 'fore your Troopers rearranged his teeth. In this one, you can see three Troopers kickin' the shit outta this Negro as he lies on the ground. How would you describe that picture?

GOVERNOR WALLACE   Maybe they were provoked. They're only human, you know.

LBJ   That's right, *they're all only human.* If you really don't want this march, you could shut it off in a minute. Why don't you instruct Alabama counties to register these voters?

GOVERNOR WALLACE   Counties are locally run. I haven't got the political power to do that.

LBJ   You had the power to keep the President off the ballot last year; surely you can tell a few county registrars what's what.

GOVERNOR WALLACE   Under Alabama law they're independent.

LBJ   Then why don't you *persuade* them?

GOVERNOR WALLACE   I don't think that's possible, Mr. President, they're pretty close with their authority.

LBJ   Don't shit me about your persuasive powers, George. Why just this mornin' I was watchin' you on TV and you were attackin' me.

GOVERNOR WALLACE   Not you, Mr. President, I was speaking against Federal Intervention . . .

LBJ bores in on Wallace, squashing him back in his chair like a bug.

LBJ   . . . you was attackin' me, George, and you were so damn persuasive I had to turn off the set 'fore you had me changin' my mind! Why are you doin' all this stuff, George? You come into office a liberal—just like me. You were tryin' to do things for the poor—just like me. So, why are you suddenly off on this Negro thing?

I got all kinds of bills I'm workin' on to help poor people. Let's you and me show these Harvard know-it-alls how a couple of country boys can get things done. Now, you're a smart fella, and I know you're already thinkin' ahead to 1968 . . .

GOVERNOR WALLACE   . . . that's not true, Mr. President . . .

LBJ   . . . Bullshit, George, you're just like me, you'll run 'till you drop but what you ought to be doin' is thinkin' about *1988*. You and me will be cold in the ground by then and the question is, what do you want left after you die? You want a great big ole marble monument that reads, "George Wallace—He Built!" Or you want a little piece of scrubby pine board lyin' across the caliche soil that says, "George Wallace—He Hated." So, you gonna protect those people as they march? We gotta deal?

GOVERNOR WALLACE   A deal?

LBJ   You're gonna authorize the State of Alabama to protect King and those marchers, and me and the Federal government is gonna stay out of it, and then the nigras is gonna go home happy and outta our hair, and you and me is gonna tend to the real business of government.

GOVERNOR WALLACE (*overwhelmed*) I guess, we'll—we'll do what we can.

LBJ grabs Wallace by the arm and pulls him to his feet.

LBJ Good! Now, let's you and I go face those press fellas and you can tell 'em about the historic decision we been making.

ALL the Witnesses rise as Reporters, shouting and calling out. Camera flashes exploding.

LBJ Ladies and gentlemen. I'm here to tell you, the ghost of Lincoln is walkin' up and down the halls of the White House pretty regularly these days! But I know you didn't come here today to hear me talk; you want to hear the announcement that Governor Wallace of Alabama is gonna make. Governor?

Wallace is sweating bullets, trying to figure a way out of this box.

GOVERNOR WALLACE The, uh, the President was a gentleman, as he always is. And I hope I was a gentleman, too.

LBJ Tell 'em what we talked about, Governor; tell 'em what we agreed to.

GOVERNOR WALLACE Well, we had a, a frank, a very frank and friendly discussion. I do appreciate the courtesy of the President.

LBJ And about the march. Tell 'em *what you decided about that.*

GOVERNOR WALLACE And I uh, I told the President, regardin' the Marchers ... that the State of Alabama—just can't *afford* to provide that kinda protection. We just don't have the money.

LBJ stares coldly at Wallace—absorbing his public betrayal.

LBJ So, that bein' the case ... (*to Press*) I certainly appreciate the Governor's keen sense of financial responsibility and so, in response to Governor Wallace's *personal request*, I have reluctantly agreed to federalize the Alabama National Guard. Dr. King will have his march and the State of Alabama will guarantee their security!

Wallace is stunned. LBJ raises his hand in the air, like they were campaigning together.

LBJ   THANK YOU, LADIES AND GENTLEMEN, THAT WILL BE ALL!

PRESS leaves. Wallace exits with Trammel.

GOVERNOR WALLACE (*quietly*)   Goddamn, get me the hell outta here, Seymore, 'fore he announces I'm in favor of Civil Rights!

LIGHTS SHIFT.

TB: ***HOUSE OF REPRESENTATIVES. MARCH 15, 1965. VIETNAM: 511 AMERICAN DEAD. 1,517 WOUNDED.***
LBJ addresses Congress.

LBJ   Today, I deliver my Voting Rights Bill to Congress. Rarely does an issue lay bare the heart of America itself. There is no Negro problem. There is no Southern problem. There is only an American problem—the failure of America to live up to its unique founding purpose—all men are created equal. There is no constitutional issue here; the command of the constitution is plain. There is no moral issue. It is wrong to deny your fellow Americans the right to vote. There is no issue of state's rights; there is only the issue of human rights. This time, there must be no delay, no hesitation, and no compromise. The real hero of this struggle is the American Negro. His actions and protests, his courage to risk safety and even to risk his life have awakened the conscience of this nation. Their cause must be our cause, too, because it is not just Negroes, but really it is all of us, who must overcome the crippling legacy of bigotry and injustice. *And—we—shall overcome!*

As the realization spreads that LBJ has used the signature phrase of the Civil Rights Movement, there is growing, rapturous applause.

Applause CUTS OFF. LIGHT SHIFT. LBJ alone with MLK except for Hoover who watches from a spot US.

MLK   A shining moment, Mr. President.

LBJ I told you, Dr. King—we're in this together.

MLK (*smiling*) Yes, sir, you did.

They shake hands.

What an enormous difference this will make in the South.

LBJ Yes, it will.

MLK Now, perhaps, we should move our focus to the North.

A moment.

LBJ (*surprised*) The North?

MLK To the urban poor. The ghetto.

A moment.

LBJ You know how a rattlesnake eats a rat?

Bewildered, MLK shakes his head.

Well, it's the damndest thing. He just unhinges his jaws and swallows him whole—teeth and claws and tail. But it takes him awhile to digest. And during that time, while he's digesting, he just sits quiet and thanks God for His blessings.

LBJ leaves. MLK notices Hoover. Hoover leaves. LIGHTS SHIFT. A Street. LA. Two CALIFORNIA HIGHWAY PATROL OFFICERS drag in a young Black man, MARQUETTE FRYE, and take a bottle from him. A Crowd begins to gather around.

CHP#1 You drunk, boy?

MARQUETTE FRYE That's California orange juice, Officer. From the Golden State!

CHP#2 More vodka than OJ.

MARQUETTE FRYE I been celebratin' my discharge from the Air Force. No Vietnam for me; I'm a free man!

CHP#2 You know the drill—walk the line!

MARQUETTE FRYE   Yessir!

Frye struts a straight line; does a fancy spin finish.

Would ya like to see me do it BACKWARDS!

The CROWD laughs. The CHP Officers get nervous. One draws his SHOTGUN.

CHP#1   STEP BACK! THIS IS POLICE BUSINESS! CUFF'EM!

CHP#2 cuffs Frye's hands.

MARQUETTE FRYE   Why you gotta do that, man; I AIN'T DONE SHIT!

CHP#2   SHUT THE FUCK UP, MONKEY!

MARQUETTE FRYE   THIS IS BULLSHIT! I AIN'T GOIN' NOWHERE!

CHP#2 clubs Frye.

CHP#2   IN THE CAR!!

CHP#1   GET'EM IN THE CAR! LET'S GO!

The Troopers, dragging Frye, retreat, with the crowd following.

CROWD   FUCK YOU, WHITEY!/LET'EM GO!/KILL THE PIGS! KILL THE PIGS! KILL THE PIGS!!

CHP#1 cocks his shotgun; aims at crowd.

CHP#1 *(terrified)*   CALL FOR BACKUP! *CALL FOR BACKUP!!*

SOUND of glass breaking, sirens, and approaching helicopters.

TB reads: **WATTS, CALIFORNIA.**

BLACKOUT.

END OF ACT ONE.

ACT TWO

TB: *Images of smouldering LA post-riot.*

The Set has been partially vandalized. There is smoke in the air. LBJ stands USC, in a SPOT, surveying the wreckage.

LBJ   I keep dreamin' about that plane, the one I was supposed to be on. World War II, I flew as an observer on a B-17 makin' a bombin' run in New Guinea. I walked off my assigned plane in Garbutt Field to take a leak and when I got back, some other officer had grabbed my place as a joke so I jumped on another plane. We flew through a blizzard of anti-aircraft fire and Jap Zeroes and just barely made it back alive and they gave me the Silver Star. But the plane I was supposed to be on? That one got shot down and everybody on it died, their bodies still rotting back there in the jungle. I keep dreamin' about that plane. We're approachin' the target and suddenly outta nowhere we get attacked by these three Jap Zeroes, their bullets smashin' into us like pile drivers. I can feel the plane shudder and slow down as first one and then two engines quit working. Thick black smoke fills the cabin, choking me. I can feel the heat. See flames.

Black Rioters enter, quietly chanting "Burn, baby, burn!" TB reads: **WATTS, CALIFORNIA. AUGUST 11, 1965.**

The pilot is screamin' we gotta jump but there are no parachutes. None. I can't find a parachute anywhere. I'm standin' there trying to choose. Do I jump out and die, or stay in the plane and burn alive? What do I do? What do I do?

LIGHTS SHIFT. CHANT soars in Volume. TB reads: **VIETNAM: 1,086 AMERICAN DEAD; 3,324 WOUNDED.**

MLK climbs up onto the President's desk and tries to get the attention of the crowd. In the OVAL OFFICE, LBJ and Humphrey watch on TV.

MLK   All over America, Negroes must join hands and . . .

MALE RIOTER#1   . . . AND BURN!

MLK   . . . And work together in a creative way.

LBJ   Thirty-four people dead.

MALE RIOTER#4   Where's the Mayor?!

LBJ   Thousands injured.

FEMALE RIOTER#1   The Mayor should come down here himself and see how we're living!

LBJ   Six hundred buildings burned.

MALE RIOTER#2   HE'LL BURN THE MOST!

LBJ   AND FOR WHAT!

MALE RIOTER#3   Man, that son of a bitch ain't gonna come to Watts; he can't get his big-assed air-conditioned Cadillac down here!

MLK   I promise you, I will do everything in my power to get the Mayor to come talk with you. *(wryly)* And I know you will be courteous to him.

Howls of laughter from the Rioters.

VICE PRESIDENT HUBERT HUMPHREY   Those people are in despair, Mr. President.

LBJ   And burning their own neighborhood helps?!

MLK   I know the conditions you live in are deplorable but I believe in non-violence . . .

FEMALE RIOTER#1   We not gonna turn that other cheek no more!

MALE RIOTER#1   WE'RE NOT GONNA LIVE LIKE THIS ANYMORE; CAGED UP IN HERE LIKE ANIMALS!

VICE PRESIDENT HUBERT HUMPHREY   Maybe they don't feel it is their neighborhood.

MALE RIOTER#2   WE GONNA TEAR UP LOS ANGELES!

MLK   I'm here because wherever we are—Selma, Birmingham, or Los Angeles—we are brothers and sisters! WE ALL GO UP TOGETHER, OR WE GO DOWN TOGETHER!

LIGHTS SHIFT. MLK joins LBJ, Humphrey, and now Hoover.

Watts was a desperate cry for help.

LBJ   The only people this helps are Dirksen and his bunch. They're lookin' for anyway they can to discredit and scandalize my programs and Watts is all the ammunition they need. A man has no more right to destroy property with a Molotov cocktail in Los Angeles, than the Ku Klux Klan has to go out and hurt people in Alabama!

MLK   That's not fair, Mr. President. These people have nothing . . .

LBJ   . . . The Federal Government is pourin' millions of dollars into poverty programs . . . !

MLK   . . . which local authorities are diverting for their own patronage machines. The money is not getting to the people who need it!

LBJ glances at Humphrey.

LBJ   It's possible there are a few hiccups; Rome wasn't built in a day.

MLK   But it can be burned down in one. Several Democratic Senators have complained publicly about the same problem.

LBJ   "Several Democratic Senators." Would that be, maybe, I don't know, Bobby Kennedy?

MLK   Yes, he was one of them . . .

LBJ *(to Humphrey)*   . . . Bobby Kennedy . . !

MLK *(quickly)*   The point is, if you move your poverty funds in Los Angeles to where they are truly needed . . .

LBJ   . . . Hubert, you get things going down there, everything we got—money, marbles, and chalk! (*back to MLK*) But you need to calm people down! Congress has already cut funding of my poverty programs in half. *In half.* And they're not done; they can smell the midterms. I'm doing everythin' I can to stop the bleedin' but it's damn hard to make the case Congress should restore monies to people who are just gonna burn it up.

MLK   People resort to violence only when they feel there are no other solutions.

VICE PRESIDENT HUMPHREY   We are doin' everything we can . . .

MLK   . . . Legislatively, yes, but if the Government won't *enforce* its own laws, what is the point? We succeeded in Selma by working together, combining local activism with Federal action. That's the approach we should take to major urban areas like Los Angeles. Or Chicago.

LBJ (*carefully*)   Chicago?

MLK   Chicago's much worse then Los Angeles and not just in the misallocation of Poverty funds. It's everything. Your excellent Education bill directed millions of dollars to our chronically underfunded black schools but Mayor Daley sent those monies to white schools. Local activists are suing Chicago right now but the Federal government is strangely silent. Why is that?

LBJ   I can't intervene in a Court case.

MLK   You don't need a court order to *with-hold funds* from cities which don't abide by Federal rules.

LBJ   You want me to cut Daley's funding?

MLK   I want you to encourage his compliance with the law. It's a very big stick, Federal funding. You use it in the South; why not Chicago?

LBJ   Dick Daley has been a great friend to Civil Rights. We'd have never gotten either the '64 or the '65 Bill without the fourteen Congressional votes he controls.

MLK   He certainly seems in favor of Civil Rights in the South; just not so much in Illinois.

LBJ   Challenge Daley and you will lose his support.

MLK   Ignoring the problems of the ghetto is not a solution; that is the lesson of Los Angeles!

LBJ   The lesson of Los Angeles is how quickly we can lose everything we've gained! Don't do this, Dr. King.

A moment.

MLK   Mr. President.

MLK leaves.

LBJ   Daley is gonna shit a brick.

VICE PRESIDENT HUMPHREY   Chicago *is* a problem.

LBJ   I know, I know! Daley and all the rest of these Big City Bosses, they still do things the old way. They'll change, they have to, but these things take time.

VICE PRESIDENT HUMPHREY   Bobby Kennedy is threatening to hold public hearings.

LBJ   Little Joe McCarthy. I'll deal with Bobby when the time comes. Less than a fucking year 'til the midterms and King wants to start a campaign in *Illinois?* What the hell is wrong with these people! Get things runnin' in LA, and keep an eye on Bobby's committee. I'll see what I can do with Daley.

Humphrey leaves. Hoover places a file folder on the desk.

J. EDGAR HOOVER   Regarding the riots; not everything was as "spontaneous" as King would have you believe. Stanley Levison is back in King's inner circle.

LBJ (*accusingly*)   You said King had dumped Levison.

J. EDGAR HOOVER   That's what King said; obviously he lied to us. *These riots were not accidental.*

LBJ (*skeptical*)   Communists?

J. EDGAR HOOVER   Hard to fight a war abroad when you're fighting a war at home.

A moment.

LBJ   Keep an eye on'em.

*LIGHTS SHIFT. UP on King/Bevel, Abernathy and **LEVISON** at the steps of the LINCOLN MEMORIAL.*

RALPH ABERNATHY   . . . Chicago's not worth it! We could lose LBJ's support completely. Martin?

MLK   He wasn't happy about Selma either, but he came around.

JAMES BEVEL   Why are we always tiptoeing around LBJ? Whether it's Chicago or Vietnam . . .

RALPH ABERNATHY   . . . Don't get started on Vietnam again.

JAMES BEVEL   Who's dying over there? *Young black men.*

MLK   You're not wrong, Jim . . .

STANLEY LEVISON   . . . but Vietnam is not our focus right now.

JAMES BEVEL   Fine. It should be, but fine. OK, Chicago. We've spent months getting this ready and we shouldn't chicken out just 'cause it's not convenient for LBJ. Local leadership is in place. Excited. Chicago is good to go.

RALPH ABERNATHY   Are *we*? We're the *Southern* Christian Leadership Conference and the North is a whole different kettle of fish.

MLK   I don't disagree.

RALPH ABERNATHY   This is a huge step up for us, Martin. Chicago's a hundred times bigger than Selma . . .

JAMES BEVEL   . . . and just as segregated.

STANLEY LEVISON   Or worse.

RALPH ABERNATHY   But Daley is no Sheriff Clark; he's *smart*. And he runs Chicago like his private kingdom.

MLK   We can't sit still; the ground is shifting under our feet. All we've done is raise people's expectations but if we don't start delivering real progress they can see and feel, Watts will only be the beginning. (*Beat*) We have to go to Chicago.

> *LIGHTS SHIFT. CHICAGO. In one spot,* **MAYOR DALEY** *faces a crowd of Reporters; in another spot, MLK faces the same crowd of reporters.*

CHICAGO REPORTERS   Mayor Daley!/Dr. King!/Mayor!/Over here, Dr. King!/Mayor!

CHICAGO REPORTER#1   What do you say to Dr. King's announcement that the SCLC will begin a new campaign here?!

MAYOR DALEY (*smiling broadly*)   Welcome to Chicago! Hope you brought a coat, it gets pretty darn cold here in the winter.

CHICAGO REPORTER#2   Why are you in Chicago, Dr. King?

MLK   Because blocks from here, Negroes live in rat-infested slums with no electricity and no heat.

CHICAGO REPORTER#5   King says a lot of tough things about slums in Chicago.

MAYOR DALEY   We have no slums in Chicago, alright.

MLK   And Mayor Daley . . .

MAYOR DALEY   What we got is some bad housing.

MLK   Mayor Daley seems indifferent to their suffering.

MAYOR DALEY   And we're doing everything we can to make sure our landlords are good citizens.

MLK Mayor Daley only seems to notice the Negroes of Chicago at Election time when he expects our votes.

CHICAGO REPORTER#4 King says Chicago is the problem!

CHICAGO REPORTER#5 Daley says there is no problem!

MAYOR DALEY I'm sure Dr. King means well.

MLK I'm sure Mayor Daley's heart is in the right place.

MAYOR DALEY But with all due respect, I don't think he really knows what he's talking about.

MLK But with all due respect, I don't think he really knows what he's talking about.

LIGHTS SHIFT to OVAL OFFICE. LBJ and Daley on the phone.

MAYOR DALEY What the hell is this clown doing in my city?!

LBJ Calm down, Dick.

MAYOR DALEY He's organized demonstrations, boycotts, even moved his own family into one of the projects in Lawndale, although before he arrived he made damn sure his gang cleaned and painted the apartment. Now I tell people, you wanta do slum clearance? Move Dr. King and his family around, one apartment at a time! Just this morning, he marched to City Hall and nailed his Demands to the door!

LBJ Well, his name is Martin Luther.

MAYOR DALEY You gotta do something about this!

LBJ No, *you gotta do something about it.* We're trying to turn things around and Chicago has got its share, some say more than its share, of Federal monies but they aren't getting to the people who need'em! That's why King is there.

MAYOR DALEY What're you saying? *I'm stealing?!*

LBJ I'm not saying that but seventy percent of the Poverty funds in your town are going to salaries for patronage jobs.

MAYOR DALEY   I'm not supposed to take care of my people?

LBJ   You're supposed to take care of *all* the people.

MAYOR DALEY   Well forgive me for being loyal to the people who been loyal to me but for all your bitching about Chicago you certainly don't have any problem with us when you want our votes.

LBJ   I'm not gonna step in there, Dick; he's got some legitimate issues. You want King outta your hair? Fix your problems!

LBJ hangs up. LIGHTS SHIFT. WHITE HOUSE SITUATION RM. LBJ, McNamara, Humphrey, **JOHN MCCONE, CIA DIRECTOR***. LBJ holds up a red briefing folder.*

This is the best we can do? Thirty-four air strikes and we lost how many planes?

ROBERT MCNAMARA   Twenty-five.

JOHN MCCONE   And the South Vietnamese lost six.

LBJ   And how much damage did we inflict?

ROBERT MCNAMARA   According to General Wheeler, we've not reduced their overall military capabilities, if anything, the strikes have only hardened their attitudes.

LBJ   What other options does that leave us?

A moment.

ROBERT MCNAMARA   Ground troops.

LBJ   Ground troops. John, what do your analysts over at Langely think?

JOHN MCCONE   We don't see expanding into a full-scale ground war as likely to improve the situation, indeed, it could become much worse. We could find ourselves mired down in a combat that we cannot win.

ROBERT MCNAMARA   In all fairness, the CIA record in predicting military outcomes has not been sterling.

JOHN MCCONE   The scenario to worry about here is not the Bay of Pigs but Korea!

LBJ   Thank you, John.

JOHN MCCONE   Mr. President.

McCone leaves.

LBJ   It's like I'm standing on a piece of newspaper in the middle of the Atlantic Ocean. If I go this way, I'll topple over. And if I go that way, I'll topple over. And if I stay where I am, the paper will be soaked up and I will sink slowly to the bottom of the sea.

ROBERT MCNAMARA   There is no question that current policy can only lead to defeat. We have to take more aggressive action.

VICE PRESIDENT HUMPHREY   Meaning what?

ROBERT MCNAMARA   We should increase our ground presence by forty thousand troops . . .

VICE PRESIDENT HUMPHREY   Forty thousand!

ROBERT MCNAMARA   Mobilize the National Guard.

LBJ   Not the Guard; that'll play hell with the economy.

ROBERT MCNAMARA (*nodding*)   OK, a draft increase but we should be pressing the fight against the VC, running them to ground and destroying them.

VICE PRESIDENT HUMPHREY   You are suggesting we move from a strictly defensive posture of air strikes to a policy of *offensive action?*

ROBERT MCNAMARA   "Search and destroy."

LBJ   You wouldn't want to call it that.

ROBERT MCNAMARA   "Aggressive Patrolling?"

VICE PRESIDENT HUMPHREY (*to McNamara*)   Did you hear what McCone said? (*to LBJ*) A land war in Asia would be ruinous to everything we're trying to do. It's what we ran against.

LBJ   The situation has changed! And if we put the Viet Cong back on their heels, it might help the new South Vietnamese government and buy us a little breathin' room here at home.

ROBERT MCNAMARA   And finally drive the Viet Cong to the negotiating table.

Sally enters.

SALLY CHILDRESS   Gardner Ackley, sir, Council of Economic Advisors.

LBJ   Hell's bells. *TWO MINUTES!* (*to McNamara*) What are we talkin' about exactly?

Sally leaves.

ROBERT MCNAMARA   An increase in both CIA and Army actions, the deployment of four Army divisions, plus one Marine air squadron, and a change in their overall mission . . .

LBJ   No. *Not "change."*

ROBERT MCNAMARA   An "Intensification?"

LBJ   I don't know what that means.

ROBERT MCNAMARA   Isn't that the point?

LBJ   The point is not to draw attention.

ROBERT MCNAMARA   "Broadening?"

LBJ (*nods approvingly*)   "A broadening of their mission . . ."

ROBERT MCNAMARA   And an—*ascending tempo* of air support?

LBJ   We want to avoid any premature publicity.

ROBERT MCNAMARA   I understand.

LBJ   No, you don't. Let's get this underway ASAP but the important thing is, these movements should be understood as *wholly consistent* with existing policy.

VICE PRESIDENT HUMPHREY   But it *is* a change in policy.

LBJ   You want to tell Congress that? You wanta see all the rest of the Great Society killed, 'cause that's what it will mean.

VICE PRESIDENT HUMPHREY   How can you hide it? The cost is . . . (*to McNamara*) How much are we talking about? Roughly.

ROBERT MCNAMARA   One and a half to two billion dollars.

LBJ   Jesus.

VICE PRESIDENT HUMPHREY   *There won't be any money for anything else.*

   ACKLEY *enters.*

GARDNER ACKLEY   Mr. President.

LBJ   Gardner! Sorry to keep you waiting. You know the Secretary of Defense?

GARDNER ACKLEY   Mr. Secretary. This is actually very fortuitous . . .

LBJ   . . . What can I do for the CEA?

GARDNER ACKLEY   It's the end of year budget projections, sir. As you know, I've been trying to get a handle on the military side for weeks now and it's been very challenging to get someone to sit down and talk with me.

LBJ   Robert, why don't you fill him in?

   A moment.

ROBERT MCNAMARA   Well, we had anticipated some budget increase along the lines of, possibly—a billion dollars . . .

GARDNER ACKLEY   A billion?

ROBERT MCNAMARA (*quickly*)   But that was before this latest round of base closures and I think, the good news is, I think when all is said and done, we will be very close to netting out zero in any real world cost basis.

GARDNER ACKLEY   So no real expansion past the current estimates?

ROBERT MCNAMARA (*carefully*)   You could say that.

LBJ   Just to be on the safe side, Gardner, I've also been thinking of going to Congress and asking for a one-time special budget request for the war, a modest supplement, six to seven hundred million dollars; something like that.

GARDNER ACKLEY   But no more?

LBJ   You know how tetchy Wilbur Mills can be with the purse strings.

ROBERT MCNAMARA (*to Gardner*)   Why don't we go over to Defense and I'll walk you through my numbers a little bit more thoroughly. If that's alright with you, Mr. President?

LBJ   Of course.

GARDNER ACKLEY   Mr. President.

LBJ   Gardner.

McNamara leaves with Ackley.

VICE PRESIDENT HUMPHREY   A special budget request to Congress?

LBJ   "To halt communist aggression." Let the bastards vote against that.

VICE PRESIDENT HUMPHREY   But the real budget problem—Mr. President, there is no way in the long run to keep this a secret and attempting to do so will only undercut your credibility.

LBJ   It will only be a problem if people like you can't keep your mouth shut.

VICE PRESIDENT HUMPHREY   You don't have to worry about my loyalty . . .

LBJ   . . . That's exactly what I worry about. You got that goddamn Minnesota Running Water Disease; can't keep from flapping your gums.

VICE PRESIDENT HUMPHREY   I'm just saying if you are going to go down this road, we should fully inform Congress.

LBJ   *The decision has been made!* That's all you need to know. Jesus Christ, if I wanted somebody to second guess me all the time and stab me in the back I'd have Bobby fuckin' Kennedy in here!

VICE PRESIDENT HUMPHREY   Mr. President, we're in this together . . .

LBJ   . . . The hell we are . . .

VICE PRESIDENT HUMPHREY   . . . "Johnson and Humphrey" . . .

LBJ   . . . Where the hell did you get that idea?! There is no WE in this, there is just ME! *The President.* And you will do as I say or you will find yourself swabbin' toilets over at the Pentagon with a goddamn Q-tip! If you're so worried about Congress, get your ass over there and shut down Bobby's committee!

VICE PRESIDENT HUMPHREY   Mr. President . . .

LBJ   GO ON! GET OUTTA HERE! GO!

SPOT OUT on LBJ. Humphrey is joined by **MURIEL**.

VICE PRESIDENT HUMPHREY   He's cut me out of the loop on Vietnam! I'm suddenly persona non grata.

MURIEL HUMPHREY   You had to tell him the truth.

VICE PRESIDENT HUMPHREY   I went back to my office and half my staff had been dismissed.

MURIEL HUMPHREY   He doesn't mean it. Let me have a quiet word with Lady Bird . . .

VICE PRESIDENT HUMPHREY . . . One of my Secret Service detail told me he thought my phone was being tapped.

MURIEL HUMPHREY Jesus.

VICE PRESIDENT HUMPHREY (*nodding*) Did you see his press conference? He insisted there was no change in Vietnam policy, or in the budget. He's not just whistling past the graveyard—he's lying. It will destroy everything we've tried to build, the whole Great Society.

MURIEL HUMPHREY You can't do anybody any good stuck in Siberia. *Lyndon needs your council.*

VICE PRESIDENT HUMPHREY (*nodding*) I've got to get back inside.

MURIEL HUMPHREY Whatever it takes.

LIGHT SHIFT. WHITE HOUSE LAWN. LBJ and Senator Bobby Kennedy.

SENATOR BOBBY KENNEDY I'm confused, Mr. President, we've constantly been told there are more than enough funds in the current budget to pay for the war, so why all of a sudden this special request?

LBJ The situation is fluid; it seemed prudent to give ourselves a little leeway.

SENATOR BOBBY KENNEDY Some people have suggested that this is really a kind of de facto congressional endorsement, after the fact, of a decision on your part to seriously escalate the war.

LBJ Well, Senator, I hope anybody who feels that way will have the guts to stand up in public and vote against it.

To Senator Bobby Kennedy's surprise, Hoover walks in.

J. EDGAR HOOVER Mr. President.

SENATOR BOBBY KENNEDY What's he doing here?

LBJ I asked the Director to join us. You don't mind, do you?

SENATOR BOBBY KENNEDY Is questioning your budget now a National Security issue?

LBJ I'm trying to do you a favor.

SENATOR BOBBY KENNEDY A favor?

LBJ Yes. It's these Committee Hearings you've been holding on my Poverty programs. You're very critical of what we're trying to do.

SENATOR BOBBY KENNEDY (*wary*) Like Dr. King . . .

At the mention of "King," LBJ and Hoover exchange looks.

SENATOR BOBBY KENNEDY . . . I'm concerned that the people for whom those programs were designed are being deliberately cut out of the management of their funds, particularly in big cities like Chicago.

LBJ Jay.

J. EDGAR HOOVER Mayor Daley has legitimate concerns that those monies will wind up in the hands of subversives.

SENATOR BOBBY KENNEDY "Subversives." No disrespect to Mayor Daley but being poor, black, and a follower of Dr. King doesn't automatically make you a subversive.

J. EDGAR HOOVER I'm surprised to hear you say that—you weren't always such a fan of Dr. King's. Certainly not when you were the Attorney General and signing off on our surveillance efforts.

A moment.

SENATOR BOBBY KENNEDY What are you worried about here, revolution in the streets? (*to LBJ*) Or a threat to your re-election campaign in '68?

LBJ I just don't want those Hearings to come back and bite you in the ass.

SENATOR BOBBY KENNEDY Oh, you're protecting me. Or is it, Mayor Daley you're protecting? Or yourself?

LBJ I'm protecting the Democratic party. Midterms are months away and your Hearings give Republicans ammunition to attack the social programs we both want. *I expect you to wrap those hearings up soon.* You understand me?

A moment. Bobby nods.

SENATOR BOBBY KENNEDY   I think I do.

LBJ   Whatever minor differences you and I might have, Party unity is what matters. (*Bobby laughs.*) Did I say something funny, Senator?

SENATOR BOBBY KENNEDY   "Party Unity." I don't know what it is but those words always sound funny coming out of your mouth. Mr. President.

Bobby walks off. LIGHTS shift. BLUE ROOM. WHITE HOUSE. LBJ/Dirksen playing cards.

LBJ   Everett, I want to thank you for your support for my Vietnam supplement; I wish all *Democrats* shared your patriotism.

SENATOR EVERETT DIRKSEN   You can't give Communists an inch, Mr. President—that's the great lesson of the last forty years. Some of our younger colleagues have forgotten that.

LBJ   Amen! Now I need you to stand shoulder to shoulder with me again, this time on restoring my Poverty funds. The Dixiecrats are gonna try to block me at every turn but if we are gonna get through this summer without any more of these riots, we've got to take care of the mess in our cities.

SENATOR EVERETT DIRKSEN   "The War on Poverty." Why don't you just call your programs, "Motherhood," or "Angel Babies," and be done with it.

LBJ   Oh, come on, Ev . . .

SENATOR EVERETT DIRKSEN   . . . I'm serious. Nobody's in favor of poverty but decent people can have legitimate differences over the solution and I don't think just throwing more Federal money at the problem is the answer. Neither does Bobby Kennedy.

LBJ   Bobby finished his hearings with a strong statement of support for our programs.

SENATOR EVERETT DIRKSEN   Let me guess, you have a little "come to Jesus" meeting with Bobby?

LBJ   As you say, decent people—legitimate differences.

SENATOR EVERETT DIRKSEN   Did Lyndon Johnson just describe Bobby Kennedy as "decent people?" The apocalypse may be upon us! Look, your whole Great Society is full of legislation sounding as wholesome as blueberry pie but it's full of mischief. *And the cost.*

LBJ   You don't think a riot is expensive? Chicago goes up in flames, you'll be the first one there with his hand out.

SENATOR EVERETT DIRKSEN   Even if I agreed with you, where is all this money coming from? And on top of the war now? I'll always support our Troops but you got to draw the line somewhere. Wilbur Mills has been working through your budget . . .

LBJ   . . . Wilbur Mills . . .

SENATOR EVERETT DIRKSEN   . . . and he says the numbers just don't add up.

LBJ   No tax increase! How many times do I have to say that?

SENATOR EVERETT DIRKSEN   Then what are you cutting? You've got to cut something, Mr. President, you can't have both guns and butter.

LBJ   What we can't do is go *backwards*, Ev. You're the only one on your side of the aisle with the vision to understand the change that's underway. That's why I depend on you; why the country depends on you. We're fighting' multiple wars here, and we've got to be united.

   A moment.

SENATOR EVERETT DIRKSEN   I'll think about it.

TB reads: **JUNE 16, 1966. GREENWOOD, MISSISSIPPI VIETNAM: 5,402 AMERICAN DEAD. 22,370 WOUNDED.**

LIGHTS SHIFT. A raucous Crowd gathers around a modest stage. It's hot and people are tense. Stokely, Levison, and Abernathy watch MLK take the mike as the Crowd calls out the traditional SCLC chant.

CROWD   FREEDOM NOW! FREEDOM NOW! FREEDOM NOW! FREEDOM NOW!

MLK   As soon as I heard about this latest act of terror against our people here in Mississippi, I left Chicago to stand beside you. I know a lot of people are saying maybe non-violence doesn't work anymore but I don't believe that. I know a lot of people are saying we should arm ourselves. That is absurd! George Wallace is always happy to see a riot because the minute we turn to violence we have *lost*! Yes, the Oppressor never willingly gives up his power; yes, Freedom must be demanded; but violence is never the solution!

Stokely can't contain himself; grabs the microphone from MLK.

STOKELY CARMICHAEL   Don't talk to me about Freedom! That Statue of Liberty bullshit. I've been arrested twenty-seven times including this morning and I ain't goin' to jail no more! I don't think we should be waiting on that cat Johnson to fix things. Johnson doesn't care about us, except as cannon fodder! He wants to ship us off to Vietnam! *Well no Viet Cong ever called me nigger!* Negroes should stay home from Vietnam and fight for black power here. You hear me?! *Fight for it.* The time for waiting has come to an end. The time for running has come to an end. You tell these white folks here in Mississippi that all the scared niggers are dead! We've been saying "Freedom!" for six years. What we're gonna start saying now is, "BLACK POWER!" That's right. That's what we want, *Black Power.* We don't have to be ashamed of it. We've begged the President. We've begged the Federal government—that's all we've been doing, begging and begging, and it's time we stand up and take over! From now on when they ask you, what do you want?!

The Crowd is split. Some chant "BLACK POWER" while others, led by a very nervous Abernathy, chant "FREEDOM NOW," but very quickly the BLACK POWER faction takes over.

Stokely smiles at MLK, who grabs the microphone, angry in a way we have never seen him before.

MLK   Don't lie to yourselves! Becoming like those who abuse us is not any kind of answer! Violence is never the solution! I'm sick of it. I'm sick of violence here in the streets of America and I'm sick of violence in the jungles of Vietnam. I'm sick of all the hatred and selfishness of this world and I will not be a part of it!

CROWD (*chanting*)   BLACK POWER! BLACK POWER!

Levison enters and pulls MLK aside.

STANLEY LEVISON   We've got a problem in Chicago.

The TB *explodes in* **IMAGES of the Chicago Riots: young BLACK MEN with Molotov cocktails; heavily armed CHICAGO POLICE.** *SOUNDS of glass breaking, sniper fire, shotgun blasts, fires, police sirens, etc.*

LIGHTS SHIFT. DALEY'S OFFICE, CHICAGO. Night.

MAYOR DALEY   Lawndale and Garfield Park are tearing themselves apart! The whole West side might go up in flames. I've had to ask the fucking Governor to send in the National Guard. To my city!

MLK   I warned you!

MAYOR DALEY   Looting! Molotov cocktails! Snipers on rooftops shooting at firemen who are trying to save their buildings! Who does that? What kind of person does that?!

MLK   I warned you this would happen but you refused to listen!

An **AIDE** *hurriedly enters and hands Daley a note.*

MAYOR DALEY   *This is your fault!* We had no problems here 'till your people showed up and started teaching these gangs about violence!

Daley glances at the note.

MLK   That is ridiculous. We have been for non-violence with all our hearts! The proof of that is the hours me and my people have spent out there on the streets tonight, trying to calm things down!

MAYOR DALEY (*to Aide*)   There is no more backup! What does he think, I got extra police up my ass? Tell 'em to hold the line with what he's got!

The Aide runs out.

MLK   You got a riot because in the middle of a goddamn heat wave some Negro kids on Roosevelt Road turned on a fire hydrant to cool off and your police shut it down and put locks on it, and then arrested them when they complained!

MAYOR DALEY   Water pressure is a public safety issue.

MLK   But only in Black neighborhoods. You didn't shut down the hydrants in Italian neighborhoods, did you? You got four swimming pools in that area but three of them are "Whites Only." If you make peaceful revolution impossible, you will make violent revolution inevitable.

MAYOR DALEY   Bullshit! We've made countless reforms! We have the best rat eradication program in the country!

*Another **AIDE** runs in with a telegram. Daley tears it open.*

MLK   Those are band-aids! I need some *real* concessions!

MAYOR DALEY (*re: Telegram*)   Two thousand National Guardsmen will be here by dawn. Things calm down, we'll talk. I'll get some— shower heads on neighborhood hydrants. Portable swimming pools. But there is never any reason for violation of the law! This will not be tolerated as long as I am mayor!

Daley exits.

MLK (*disbelief*)   Portable swimming pools?

LIGHT SHIFT. OVAL OFFICE.

VICE PRESIDENT HUMPHREY   It seems the National Guard has finally started to have an effect in Chicago; calm things down.

LBJ   And on the Hill?

VICE PRESIDENT HUMPHREY   The Republicans are having a field day.

LBJ   *Dirksen?*

VICE PRESIDENT HUMPHREY   For a moment I thought we might have regained his support for restoring funds but not after this.

LBJ   Which makes Daley's votes even more important. And less likely. Christ, what a mess.

Humphrey hands LBJ some papers.

VICE PRESIDENT HUMPHREY   Not surprisingly, GOP candidates nationwide have gotten a surge in the polls. I think we need to be aggressive in response and get you out there, supporting our people.

LBJ   You think my presence is an asset now?

VICE PRESIDENT HUMPHREY   And we have to counter Nixon. He's made himself the front-runner for '68.

LBJ (*disgusted*)   Nixon. Fucking unbelievable.

McNamara enters.

ROBERT MCNAMARA   Mr. President?

VICE PRESIDENT HUMPHREY (*re: McNamara*)   Would you like me to stay?

LBJ   I don't need your help on Vietnam. See what you can do about Dirksen.

LBJ exits with McNamara. Humphrey watches him go. LIGHTS SHIFT.

KING APARTMENT. Coretta paces, tense with fear and anger.

CORETTA   BANG! The first thing we heard were these BANGS! I tried to make a joke of it; told the kids it was firecrackers. "Let's read a book," I said, and we all huddled together on the couch . . .

MLK   . . . I'm so sorry, baby . . .

CORETTA   . . . then BANG! BANG! BANG! The shots started getting closer and closer. You could hear police sirens wailing. The whine of bullets ricocheting. I could smell smoke. For a terrible moment, I thought this building was on fire! Do we jump out the window or stay here and burn up? Just then, somebody smashed the store windows across the street and some girls started screaming and the kids rushed to the window and I yelled at 'em, screamed at 'em to, "Get away from there 'fore you get your damn heads blown off!" And I grabbed 'em and we crouched down on the floor right there; Bunny sobbing 'cause she didn't know why Momma was so mad at her.

MLK   I got back as quick as I could.

CORETTA   There was a pregnant teenage girl, just four years older then Yolanda, shot to death by the police just three blocks over on Lawndale. Wasn't doin' nothing; talking with her friends. Fourteen years old.

MLK   I know; I heard.

CORETTA   What're we doing, Martin?

MLK (*struggling*)   We're trying to—we're trying to put a stop . . .

CORETTA   . . . No. What are *we* doing?

Bevel, Abernathy, and Levison enter the room.

JAMES BEVEL   We did everything we could to tamp it down, Doc, but the kids on the street just laughed at us; called us a bunch of Uncle Toms.

CORETTA   I'm taking the kids and going back to Atlanta.

Coretta leaves. An awkward silence.

STANLEY LEVISON   It's like a fucking war zone; I've never seen anything like that before in my life.

MLK looks out the window.

RALPH ABERNATHY   I said this would be a mistake! We've wasted valuable resources here and got nothing to show for it, worse than nothing—we've lost ground and now Stokely and his bunch have hijacked the movement! Fucking "Black Power" is all anybody wants to talk about now.

MLK (*bitterly*)   Black Power.

JAMES BEVEL   Chicago is failing because you refuse to accept local leadership!

RALPH ABERNATHY   Local leadership is in bed with Daley, bought and paid for! My God, we got Negro council members who would vote against Jesus if Daley told them to.

STANLEY LEVISON   There were plenty of people who tried to help but the minute they did, they'd suddenly have a problem with their power or their running water. Daley has a thousand ways to crack the whip.

JAMES BEVEL   There was no way to predict all that.

RALPH ABERNATHY   You did the advance work!

JAMES BEVEL   And what were you doing, Ralph? What have you ever done but hang onto his coat-tails?!

MLK (*sharply*)   SHUT UP, BOTH OF YOU! You want to blame somebody, blame me! Yes, the campaign is failing. Just as worrisome is this fracture in our own ranks when we most need to be united. We have to forcibly correct this deliberate misconception that the Movement and Black Power are the same thing.

STANLEY LEVISON   Stokely and his crowd are making a lot of noise because they're weak; we don't want to fall into that trap. We need to stay focused on Chicago!

MLK   We're never going to be able to make any headway with Daley.

STANLEY LEVISON   He's an extremely adept foe.

JAMES BEVEL   Like trying to get your arms around a greased pig.

RALPH ABERNATHY   If we can't make a deal with Daley, what do we do? We can't appeal to the Federal government. Not any more.

MLK (*angry*)   Yes, Ralph, I burned that bridge when I came here. *Mea Culpa.*

STANLEY LEVISON   That's not on you, Martin. LBJ always needed Daley too much to intervene.

RALPH ABERNATHY   We should cut our losses and get out while we can.

JAMES BEVEL (*sarcastic*)   Declare victory and go home?

RALPH ABERNATHY   Isn't that your solution to Vietnam?

JAMES BEVEL   It makes sense in Vietnam.

RALPH ABERNATHY   What do you suggest here, genius, more of the same?

STANLEY LEVISON   If we leave Chicago now, it will validate for the American public every criticism Daley has ever made about the Movement.

MLK   I fundamentally misunderstood the North. It's not about *improving* the ghettoes. You can't. We need to break out of these cement reservations. Why waste our time fighting over the pittance of poverty funds allocated to our broken down schools when we could just move into white neighborhoods where the schools already work.

JAMES BEVEL   Yes!

STANLEY LEVISON   We need to go right at the system.

JAMES BEVEL   Expose Daley and the whole racist structure!

As MLK works this out, we hear the SOUND of a **WHITE CROWD***, getting louder and more violent, chanting underneath the following . . .*

WHITE CROWD   WHITE POWER! WHITE POWER! WHITE POWER!

MLK   We should lead a march.

RALPH ABERNATHY   A march?

MLK   A public march through one of these lily-white neighborhoods like Skokie . . .

RALPH ABERNATHY   Or Gage Park.

MLK   Or Gage Park. And show people what we're really dealing with.

MLK links arms with Bevel, Abernathy, Levison, and others carrying signs: **"All God's children need a place to live"** *and* **"Open neighborhoods"** *etc.*

TB: AUGUST 5, 1966. GAGE PARK, ILLINOIS. Images of White Rioters.

LIGHTS SHIFT. SOUND ramps up. White Crowd surges OS carrying home-made Confederate flags and signs: **"The Only Way to End Niggers is Exterminate!,"** **"NIGGERS GO HOME!"** **"Reds, race mixers, queers, and rapists—go home!"**

([*] indicates a time jump signaled by a THUNDERCLAP and a sharp physical shift of all the Witnesses on stage.)

WHITE CROWD   TWO! FOUR! SIX! EIGHT! WE DON'T WANTA INTEGRATE! TWO! FOUR! SIX! EIGHT! WE DON'T WANTA INTEGRATE! WHITE POWER! WHITE POWER! WHITE POWER! WHITE POWER!

[*] Two white **CHICAGO POLICEMEN** *take positions in front of MLK and marchers, trying to protect them from the white crowd.*

POLICEMAN #1 & #2   STEP BACK! STEP BACK!

RIOTER #1   You nigger-loving cops! Why are you protecting those animals?

RIOTER #2   I'll never vote for fucking Daley again!

RIOTER #3   Fuck Daley!

[*] **FATHER CLEMENTS**, *a black priest, enters and crosses to Marchers. He is stalked by a* **WHITE FEMALE PROTESTOR**, *baby in her arms, who screams at him the whole time.*

FEMALE RIOTER   You dirty nigger priest! You dirty nigger priest! Go back to Africa!

RIOTER #3   WE SHOULD BURN 'EM LIKE JEWS!

The Crowd starts chanting:

CROWD   BURN 'EM LIKE JEWS! BURN 'EM LIKE JEWS! BURN 'EM LIKE JEWS!

[*]

RIOTER #2   Hey! Where's Martin Luther COON?!

Crowd laughs and begins chanting:

WHITE CROWD   WE WANT KING! WE WANT KING!

[*]

RIOTER #3   KILL KING!

WHITE CROWD   KILL KING! KILL KING! KILL KING! KILL KING!

The Crowd lunges forward, throwing rocks, bricks, bottles, and cherry bombs. A ROCK hits MLK in the head and he stumbles to his knees, blood pouring down his face.

RALPH ABERNATHY   MARTIN!

[*] *All ACTION on stage freezes—SPOT on MLK as the SOUND of the white mob is reduced to a dull roar. MLK rises slowly to his feet, staring at the audience.*

MLK   I've been in demonstrations all across the south but I have never seen—even in Mississippi and Alabama—mobs as hostile and hate-filled as I've seen in Chicago. I think the people from Mississippi ought to come to Chicago to learn how to hate!

MLK collapses. POLICE SIRENS wail.

LIGHTS up on OVAL OFFICE where LBJ, Mayor Daley, and Hoover have been watching riot footage on the TV.

MAYOR DALEY   Whose side are you on?!

LBJ   The side that doesn't stone people! I warned you about your problems, Dick. I told you to fix'em.

Freeze breaks. The stage empties of Protestors and Rioters.

MAYOR DALEY   Hey! These imported prophets of so-called "non-violence" deliberately incited people by marching through white neighborhoods!

LBJ   "White neighborhoods." That's the point.

MAYOR DALEY   People should be able to live where they want and with who they want. Since when is that a crime?

LBJ   Discrimination is a crime.

MAYOR DALEY   A man's home is his castle!

LBJ   What about his schools? His hospitals? His jobs? You won't fix Negro neighborhoods, so what choice does King have?

MAYOR DALEY   What choice do we have? For years, Chicago worked 'cause everybody got enough of what he needed to feel like he had a place at the table. And because it worked, I was able to deliver votes to Washington. King has killed all that. I got white people spitting at my cops and cursing my name and you know what?

This time they're not gonna vote the straight ticket. Midterm elections just weeks away and we're looking at serious losses, and not just in Chicago. White people all over the country are getting fed up with this violence and don't think for a second the Republicans haven't noticed. You see Nixon out there, stoking the fires? King and his gang are gonna destroy the Democratic party! Tell him that thing his Lieutenant, Stokely, said. Go on, tell him!

J. EDGAR HOOVER   "Asking Negroes to join the Democratic party is like asking Jews to join the Nazi Party."

MAYOR DALEY   "Nazis." We're Nazis now? And that's just the least of it. You should hear the things he says about you and Vietnam! You are a lot more loyal to Dr. King, than Dr. King is to you!

LBJ   What about Vietnam?

MAYOR DALEY   You didn't see his last rally? "Johnson's a killer! Johnson's a destroyer of human life!"

LBJ (*very quietly*)   King said that?

MAYOR DALEY (*to Hoover*)   Am I right?

J. EDGAR HOOVER   King is not your friend, Mr. President.

Sensing blood in the water, Daley presses his point.

MAYOR DALEY   He's a liar. Whatever King says to your face, he's against you in Vietnam. You don't run from people who've been your friends; you stick with them. We don't run. We stand with Johnson on Vietnam! And we also stand for law and order, and I'll be damned if I'll let anyone take over the running of my city!

LBJ   What shape you got King in now? Is he about ready to get out of Chicago?

MAYOR DALEY   Hell, I don't know, they live in a fantasy world!

LBJ   You gotta give him somethin', Dick . . .

MAYOR DALEY   . . . I'm not going to give that bastard shit!

LBJ   *Make it look like you're givin' him something.* You understand me? Make a deal, any kind of deal; I don't care what. You're right, Dick. We need to put an end to this and deal with the midterms.

Daley nods and leaves.

LBJ   King really said that about me?

J. EDGAR HOOVER   Everywhere King goes there's unrest and a relentless attack on you. This is Stokely at a rally with King in Greenwood, Mississippi just before the Chicago riots started . . .

Hoover turns on a TAPE RECORDER.

STOKELY CARMICHAEL (*on tape*)   "Johnson doesn't care about us, except as cannon fodder. He wants to ship us out to Vietnam! Well, no Viet Cong ever called me nigger! Negroes should stay home from Vietnam and fight for Black Power here . . . "

LBJ turns off Tape.

LBJ   "Black Power?" What the hell is that?

J. EDGAR HOOVER   Black Power is permission to riot, burn, loot, and kill. What does that have to do with Civil Rights? We have got to start fighting back before there's an all out race war! (*quietly*) For months now, we have had a very comprehensive operation in the works just waiting your word to launch. COINTELPRO. A nation-wide effort against all these Black Nationalist/Hate Groups.

LBJ   How?

J. EDGAR HOOVER   Target the leadership. Infiltrate their organizations. Set them against each other. Provoke them into actions which will give us the legal justification to respond with overwhelming force and crush them once and for all.

Sally enters.

SALLY CHILDRESS   General Westmoreland and the Secretary of Defense.

LBJ nods. Sally leaves.

LBJ   I don't care about the personal stuff. *Vietnam.* Bring me *proof* that King's against me in Vietnam and then we'll talk about your plan.

Hoover leaves as McNamara and Westmoreland enter. A moment.

LBJ   How bad is it?

GENERAL WESTMORELAND   Late yesterday afternoon, two of the Northern-most provinces were overrun by a regiment-size enemy force. In many places the ARVN simply threw down their weapons and ran away. Even more worrisome, this was the first attack we've seen by North Vietnamese Regulars.

LBJ   *The North Vietnamese Regular Army*, not the Viet Cong?

ROBERT MCNAMARA   To compound matters, we have a new regime change . . .

LBJ   . . . *Another* new regime change?

ROBERT MCNAMARA   Yes, sir. Air Force General Nguyen Cao Ky is now Prime Minister and Army General Nguyen Van Thieu is Chief of State.

LBJ   What's the word on them?

ROBERT MCNAMARA   Thieu is capable but ambitious. Ky is by all accounts an unguided missile. Drinks. Gambles. Womanizes. In Public, he wears a zipper-studded black flying suit, with a lavender ascot and twin pearl-handled revolvers engraved with the name of his favorite prostitute.

GENERAL WESTMORELAND   The absolute bottom of the barrel.

ROBERT MCNAMARA   The situation is dire, Mr. President.

LBJ   What do you suggest?

GENERAL WESTMORELAND   We strongly recommend an increase of 300,000 soldiers.

A moment.

LBJ (*shaken*)   In January of last year we had what, 23,000 troops, and in a year and a half, we will be over 300,000?

GENERAL WESTMORELAND   Closer to 375,000.

LBJ   Do we even have that?

ROBERT MCNAMARA   We would double our military call-ups; increase the draft to 35,000 a month. And we might have to— modify our standards downwards.

GENERAL WESTMORELAND   I think that's a mistake.

ROBERT MCNAMARA (*sharply*)   Unless we want to eliminate college deferments it's not a choice!

LBJ   Thank you, General. As always, I appreciate your frankness.

Westmoreland leaves.

What do you estimate the cost?

ROBERT MCNAMARA   At least twelve billion for 1966.

LBJ   *Twelve billion?* What the hell do I tell Ackley now? Or Dirksen? We can't pretend that another round of base closures is gonna fill the gap. No bullshit supplemental bill. There will have to be a tax increase.

ROBERT MCNAMARA   Not necessarily. Twelve billion is the near term cost for a war which continues indefinitely but—if we were to operate on the—hypothetical assumption that the war would be *completely over*—all our troops and material withdrawn by, say, January, 1967—a more reasonable estimate would be closer to the original one billion dollar figure that I gave Ackley two months ago.

A moment.

LBJ   And it could be.

ROBERT MCNAMARA   What could be?

LBJ   The war *could be* over by '67. I mean, the North Vietnamese could come to their senses at any moment and make a deal so, it's *possible*. Right?

ROBERT MCNAMARA   Yes, sir. It's possible.

LBJ   Congressional support for Vietnam is like the Rio Grande, Robert—wide but not very deep, and the Press is already sniffin' around, waitin' to jump on me. *We've got to get the goddamn North Vietnamese to the table.* The problem is we're not nailin' any damn coon skins to the wall. You need to kill more Viet Cong. I want a weekly report detailing the number of VC dead and I wanta see that fucking number go up.

Lady Bird enters.

LADY BIRD   Lyndon?

LBJ   What?

LADY BIRD   It's time. (*off his look*) Remember? Lynda wanted you to meet her young man,

LBJ nods. McNamara exits. Lady Bird signals and **LYNDA BIRD** *enters, clutching the arm of* **CHARLES ROBB**, *a handsome young Marine in full dress uniform.*

LYNDA BIRD   Daddy? This is Lieutenant . . .

Robb extends his hand.

LBJ   . . . Charles Robb. From Virginia, yes I know.

CHARLES ROBB   Mr. President. It's an honor, sir.

LBJ takes his hand.

LBJ   You're one of our Social Aides, yes?

CHARLES ROBB   Yes, sir, but I was hoping to change my position.

LBJ glances over at Lady Bird and Lynda.

LBJ (*wryly*)   Well, he certainly has all the makings of a politician. What can I do for you, son?

CHARLES ROBB   I would like to be sent to Vietnam, sir. Combat duty. It's what I trained for.

LBJ and Lady Bird look at one another.

REPORTERS   Mr. President! Mr. President! Mr. President!

LIGHTS SHIFT. WHITE HOUSE PRESS ROOM. LBJ faces an increasingly skeptical PRESS. Humphrey stands behind him, used to his role now as virtual stage prop.

TB reads: **SEPTEMBER, 1966. VIETNAM: 6,990 AMERICAN DEAD. 29,819 WOUNDED.**

REPORTER#1   Mr. President, it's been a brutal couple of months for your Administration—riots in Chicago, increased protests over your Vietnam policy, and a new low in your personal ratings. How do you feel about your chances in the midterm elections?

LBJ   Well you guys certainly don't help with your focus only on the bad news but I trust the American people to do the right thing and stay the course!

REPORTER#3   Despite all these setbacks, your administration seems remarkably united. Is there really no difference of opinion?

LBJ   Not that I'm aware of—but let's ask the Vice President here.

Reporters turn to a surprised Humphrey.

VICE PRESIDENT HUMPHREY   Every member of this administration is one thousand percent behind President Johnson and his policies!

LBJ nods approvingly.

And let me just say in response to your other point, that those draft dodgers out there doing these protests and marches, they dishonor our brave soldiers who are dying in Vietnam.

LIGHTS shift. LBJ and Humphrey alone.

LBJ   That was impressive what you did back there. Why don't you join me and McNamara on Tuesday?

VICE PRESIDENT HUMPHREY (*relieved*)   Yes, sir, Mr. President. I'd be delighted.

LIGHTS SHIFT. CHICAGO CITY HALL. SPOT on MLK and Daley, standing side by side at a Press Conference.

MAYOR DALEY   The City of Chicago is pleased to announce the ten-point Open Housing Summit Agreement has passed unanimously. Among other key provisions, the City of Chicago promises to agree to work for an Open Housing ordinance. And the Illinois Real Estate Board will encourage its members to obey existing laws. Dr. King?

MLK   I want to thank Mayor Daley for his willingness to engage on these very difficult issues. The Summit Agreement is a major achievement, and one that all Chicago citizens can be proud of.

MLK and Daley shake hands for photographers but as soon as the picture is taken, they separate.

Bevel and Abernathy confer quietly with MLK.

JAMES BEVEL (*urgently*)   There's nothing binding here, Doc. No real goals. No timetable. No enforcement penalties. It's just a lot of vague promises to "do better."

RALPH ABERNATHY   It's the best we could get.

JAMES BEVEL   It's meaningless!

MLK   We *lost*, James. And it wasn't just Daley. The people in Chicago don't want integration any more than Selma does.

JAMES BEVEL   What do we do then?

Beat.

MLK   I have no fucking idea.

MLK walks off. Lights shift.

TB: ***NOVEMBER 8, 1966. NEWSPAPER HEADLINES:
"MIDTERM ELECTIONS!"***

*SOUND of "HAPPY DAYS ARE HERE AGAIN" and a SPOT
on* **RICHARD NIXON** *facing a GOP Campaign HQ CROWD.
Simultaneously at the LBJ RANCH. LIVING ROOM. LBJ glumly
enters holding the phone which he dials as he watches Nixon on TV.
SONG melds into APPLAUSE.*

RICHARD NIXON   Republicans took back forty-seven members
in the House, three Senators, eight Governors, and six hundred and
seventy-seven seats in State Legislatures! This midterm election is the
greatest comeback of any political Party in the history of the Country!

APPLAUSE

And why? It's very simple: law and order. Criminals are running wild
in the streets and decent Americans are tired of having to live in fear!
Decent Americans want a government which is willing to control
these lawless elements, instead of a government which rewards them!
We hear you, America!

LBJ turns TV off. SPOT on Dirksen on phone.

LBJ   Congratulations, Ev,

SENATOR EVERETT DIRKSEN   Thank you, Mr. President.

LBJ   "Riots, Rape, and Robbery." That's the message of the
Republican party?

SENATOR EVERETT DIRKSEN   Law and Order is a very real concern.

LBJ   It's fear mongering! I never thought I'd see the day when
Everett Dirksen would kowtow to Richard Milhouse Nixon.

SENATOR EVERETT DIRKSEN   I wouldn't say "kowtow" but I
would never *count out* the former Vice President.

LBJ   No, you'd have to put a stake through his heart first.

SENATOR EVERETT DIRKSEN   He's surprisingly resilient.

LBJ   He's unnatural.

SENATOR EVERETT DIRKSEN   Whatever you think of Nixon, he's right; people are fed up.

LBJ   And the solution is to ignore the problem?

SENATOR EVERETT DIRKSEN   I warned you that you were going too fast. You've made the politician's fatal error, Mr. President, you've outrun your own constituency.

LBJ   Being out in front of the people is called *leadership*!

SENATOR EVERETT DIRKSEN   Until you take them over a cliff!

LBJ hangs up. Walks OUTSIDE to where Humphrey is sitting on the PORCH STEPS. LBJ sits beside him.

VICE PRESIDENT HUMPHREY (*quietly*)   We were up against three very popular Republican governors in big states—Romney in Michigan, Rhodes in Ohio, and this Reagan in California—that certainly could have had a lot to do with the results.

LBJ   *It's all King's fault.* You see those losses in Illinois? Hell, Daley's worried about his *own* re-election now. I warned King. I warned him! If he hadn't gone up there and stirred the pot we mighta pulled this election out but no, what do I know? I'm just the President. He's *Martin Luther King!* All those bleeding heart liberals, so eager to go to the mat for the poor Negro *except when he's in their neighborhood.* You know the difference between cannibals and liberals? Cannibals only eat their *enemies.*

VICE PRESIDENT HUMPHREY   Your re-election will be a completely different story.

LBJ (*gloomily*)   Will it? Nixon's found his issue. Wallace opened the door but racism will move beyond his cracker charm and become somethin' respectable now; even honorable. "Law and Order!" We all know what Nixon's really talkin' about—keepin' the nigger down.

VICE PRESIDENT HUMPHREY   What would you like to do, Sir?

LBJ   I have no fucking idea.

LBJ wanders back inside. SPOT on (now) Captain Robb in stained combat fatigues.

CAPTAIN CHARLES ROBB   Dear Mr. President. Again, I hope I am not taking too great a liberty in these tapes I send you. As always, I hope you and your family are well, especially my darling Lynda.

LBJ turns on a portable tape recorder and as he listens to his son-in-law, he gradually sits down.

This has been a very challenging week. My Company saw action for the first time and I lost one of my men. His name was Private Hector Elias. He was a very good Marine and well-liked. On a reconnaissance patrol, he stepped on a land mine. The Corpsman did everything he could but he died before he could be evacuated. I was there with him. (*Beat*) Nothing really prepares you for an event like that. I have tried to talk to my men about it. They understand why we are here but things are very confusing in-country. We have much in common with the Vietnamese people, a love of family and place, but they regard us with fear and distrust.

The Viet Cong are ruthless and cruel but somehow they have a support among the peasants that we lack. I don't understand this. I don't mean to burden you, who carries so much, with the late night thoughts of a Marine Officer except to say we send you our prayers and wish you wisdom in the difficult decisions you make. My love and best wishes to all of you.

Sincerely Yours, Captain Charles Robb.

The tape runs out. All we hear is the SOUND of the tape flapping.

TB reads: **VIETNAM: 8,144 AMERICAN DEAD. 34,996 WOUNDED.**

BLACKOUT.

END OF ACT TWO

ACT THREE

SPOT on LBJ facing the audience.

LBJ They were driving me to Andrew's airbase in my big custom-built Lincoln Continental, the one that's armored like a tank. There's a rally on the sidewalk and the police are trying to keep the anti-war protestors apart from this big group of construction workers. Both groups are yelling and screaming obscenities at each other with the police stuck in between. Suddenly, this girl—this girl couldn't have been but seventeen or eighteen, Luci's age, this girl she breaks through the police line and throws herself against the car. She couldn't weigh a hundred pounds soaking wet but she hits the side of the car like a linebacker, clawing the door. The windows are tinted and I know she can't really see me but I feel like she can. I feel like she's looking right at me, her eyes burning through me. The Secret Service are on her immediately but for a split-second, her face is smashed up against the window with this look—this look—this look of such hatred. Eyes rolling back in her head. Face twisted. Spit running down her chin. Blood on the glass. As she yells at me over and over again to die. Just die. Just die why don't you?

SPOT Fades OUT on LBJ.

TB reads: **MARCH, 1967. 13,170 AMERICAN DEAD. 51,043 WOUNDED.**

{From here to the end of the play, projected images will no longer be confined to the screen but will gradually begin to bleed over the Proscenium and the set itself.}

OVAL OFFICE. Ackley enters with pages of reports.

GARDNER ACKLEY Sir, we cannot contain things any longer; the cost of the war is just wreaking havoc on the economy. We could be looking at double digit inflation within the year. *We have to have a tax increase.*

LBJ (*reluctantly*) How much?

GARDNER ACKLEY A personal and corporate tax increase is essential and the sooner the better.

LBJ How much?!

GARDNER ACKLEY Ten percent.

LBJ (*shaking his head*) We could ask for maybe six percent over two years.

GARDNER ACKLEY I'm not sure six will be enough to . . .

LBJ . . . SIX PERCENT! And I'll have to strip naked on the floor of the Congress and let Mills and Dirksen beat me like a pinata to get that. If I'm lucky. *Six percent.*

    *LIGHTS SHIFT. LBJ/***MILLS***/Dirksen.*

LBJ I'm not gonna beat around the bush here, fellas, I don't like it, I don't want it, but the country needs this tax bill.

REPRESENTATIVE WILBUR MILLS Like it needs a hole in the head.

SENATOR EVERETT DIRKSEN I knew it would come to this. It's what I always said.

LBJ I never lied to you, Everett, but the situation has changed. Nobody anticipated what Vietnam would become but there it is. We're at war. You don't want to send our boys over there to fight with one hand tied behind their backs, do you?

REPRESENTATIVE WILBUR MILLS No, no, no, no, no! *This is not about patriotism.* I fully support your war effort but you need to bring your *domestic* expenses in line.

LBJ Hell's bells, Wilbur, we've recommended closing dozens of programs but you know how it is … (*pointedly at Dirksen*) … they're in so and so's district and he *needs* it.

SENATOR EVERETT DIRKSEN Congress is not responsible for this bloated domestic agenda!

REPRESENTATIVE WILBUR MILLS I told you, Ev, this was gonna be a waste of time.

LBJ Alright, alright, look, we can stand here and throw darts at each other 'till the cows come home but at the end of the day, *we gotta have a tax increase.* How do we do that?

Mills and Dirksen share a look.

REPRESENTATIVE WILBUR MILLS Well, as my Daddy used to say, to get a little, you've gotta give a little.

LBJ This isn't my first visit to the rodeo, Wilbur, what're we talkin' about?

SENATOR EVERETT DIRKSEN No more unlimited spending without commensurate cuts.

LBJ Such as?

REPRESENTATIVE WILBUR MILLS To start? A freeze on welfare payments for dependent children.

LBJ Oh, come on, Wilbur, that's unfair!

REPRESENTATIVE WILBUR MILLS If you can't balance your budget by yourself, we'll do it for you.

LBJ *Unfair to those people.* A freeze like that is gonna hurt 'em bad.

REPRESENTATIVE WILBUR MILLS Mr. President, across town from my mother in Arkansas a Negro woman has a baby every year and every time I go home my mother complains. That Negro woman's now got eleven children. My proposal will stop this. Let the states pay for more than a small number of children if they want to.

LBJ   So, your solution is to punish the children?

REPRESENTATIVE WILBUR MILLS   I gotta whole list here of cutbacks. Your tax Bill is dead unless you permanently change course.

LBJ (*very coldly*)   "Change course?"

REPRESENTATIVE WILBUR MILLS   We're not just gonna nibble around the edges and then have you come back later and blow things up again. I need a firm public commitment from you that there will be no, repeat, NO new domestic programs in fiscal 1968 and no increases in existing programs.

LBJ   Who the hell do you think you are? You don't dictate to me; I'm the President of the United States. You will rue the day you killed this Bill, both of you!

Mills and Dirksen start to leave.

LBJ   Everett, I know it doesn't add to your popularity to say we have to have additional taxes to fight this war abroad and fight our problems at home, but we can do it. *We should do it!*

Dirksen pauses at the door.

SENATOR EVERETT DIRKSEN   Mr. President, as a wise man once said to me, "Count the votes."

LIGHT SHIFT. TOMB OF THE UNKNOWN SOLDIER. LBJ and Bobby stand in a light rain, watching the GUARDS. SECRET SERVICE agents watch them. Both men speak quietly, trying to keep their feelings under wrap.

LBJ   I understand, Senator, that you recently had a "Peace Feeler" from the North Vietnamese. Not that you bothered to tell me about it, of course, I had to read it in the newspaper.

SENATOR BOBBY KENNEDY   Mr. President, I am as mystified by that story as you are. Yes, I had a courtesy meeting in France with some low-level director in their Foreign Office who seemed excited about something but the translation was hopeless and nothing seemed new about it so I ignored it. I went on to Germany, Italy . . .

LBJ . . . Met the Pope, too, I hear.

SENATOR BOBBY KENNEDY Is the Pope under suspicion, now?

LBJ Lot of travel for a Senator.

SENATOR BOBBY KENNEDY A simple fact-finding mission. All I was interested in was doing everything I could towards finding a peaceful solution to the War in Southeast Asia.

LBJ So that's why you leaked this so-called "peace feeler" to the press.

SENATOR BOBBY KENNEDY I did not leak that! I assume that came from your State Department.

LBJ It's not my State Department, Senator, it's obviously your State Department.

SENATOR BOBBY KENNEDY That's ridiculous.

LBJ Since you're on a fact-finding mission, let me give you a few facts. The war is going well. In fact, it's going so well that it could be over by this summer, provided you mind your own business!

SENATOR BOBBY KENNEDY (*incredulous*) Military victory?

LBJ That's right. So, if you keep stickin' your nose where it doesn't belong you'll be finished! I will destroy you and every one of your dove friends! You'll be dead politically in six months!

SENATOR BOBBY KENNEDY (*through gritted teeth*) If you want a peaceful settlement, stop the bombing—that's what the Europeans told me. That will shift the burden of responsibility on Hanoi.

LBJ There just isn't a chance in hell I will do that.

SENATOR BOBBY KENNEDY I'm just trying to be helpful, Mr. President.

LBJ Oh, yeah, I see that. I never want to hear your views on Vietnam again. As far as I'm concerned, you and your Dove friends are giving succor to the enemy, encouraging Hanoi to keep on fighting and keep on killing American boys. You've got blood on your hands!

SENATOR BOBBY KENNEDY Fuck you.

LIGHTS SHIFT. SENATE floor. LBJ watches Bobby.

SENATOR BOBBY KENNEDY I speak today, not to meddle in State Department business, but in the Senate's ancient and cherished obligation to stimulate debate. Three Presidents have taken action in Vietnam. If fault is to be found there is enough to go round for all—including myself—but it is clear that this Administration's policy is not going to end the war. I propose a new plan. First, test Hanoi's sincerity by extending an unconditional bombing halt and calling for negotiations. Second, begin a phased replacement of American and Communist combatants in the South by International forces. The stakes are high. There is great principle and there is also human anguish. If we can protect the one and prevent the other, then surely we must do so.

LIGHTS SHIFT. LBJ, Humphrey, Hoover.

LBJ A new plan, my ass. It's surrender! From now on, any legislative wish-list of Bobby's is dead in the water.

VICE PRESIDENT HUMPHREY This is needlessly provocative, Mr. President. It lends credence to this whole notion of a "feud." It's not helpful in the run-up to your re-election.

LBJ (*coldly*) There is no feud. We just can't afford any additional expenditures until we get this tax hike.

LIGHTS SHIFT. SCLC HQ. ATLANTA. MLK, Levison, Abernathy, and Bevel.

RALPH ABERNATHY At one time LBJ was gonna end poverty, and now Mills and Dirksen are trying to throw children off welfare to save a nickle.

JAMES BEVEL To pay for his damn war!

STANLEY LEVISON   Vietnam is just an excuse; even without it, they'd find some other way to kill his social programs.

MLK (*brooding*)   The attack is always on the most helpless; the least able to defend themselves. There is an ugly mood of violence all over this country. And abroad. A sickness. You see that article in *Ramparts* magazine, "The Children of Vietnam?" There were these— photographs. Napalm. (*Beat*) I don't think there is any difference between throwing black children out onto the street to starve and throwing jellied gasoline on yellow children in the jungles of Vietnam.

They all look at MLK.

STANLEY LEVISON (*quietly*)   This is a serious mistake, Martin.

MLK   Remaining quiet is a mistake.

JAMES BEVEL   Amen. One thousand ninety-one men killed this month alone.

MLK   James is right. It's all one thing, Stanley. This war is not just destroying our hopes for the future of this country, it is destroying its very *soul*.

RALPH ABERNATHY   SCLC's supporters never signed on for the anti-war movement.

MLK   They signed on for the non-violence movement! Do you think I should distinguish between domestic and foreign violence?

JAMES BEVEL   It's *all* wrong.

MLK   They forget that our ministry, Ralph, is in obedience to the One who loved His enemies so much He died for them.

STANLEY LEVISON   Martin, if you take a public stand against the war it will ruin any future hope of cooperation with President Johnson.

MLK   This is not personal.

RALPH ABERNATHY   You think that's how Johnson will see it?

STANLEY LEVISON   He will see it as a betrayal.

MLK   Who has betrayed whom here?! Black soldiers die on the same battleground with White soldiers for a country that won't let them live next to each other in the same neighborhood. No more compromises, Stanley. I can't do it.

SPOT on MLK. SOUNDS of enormous restive crowd.

TB reads: **APRIL 4, 1967. RIVERSIDE CHURCH, NYC. VIETNAM: 14,054 AMERICAN DEAD. 56,007 WOUNDED.**

MLK   There was a moment in this country when it seemed there was a real promise of hope for the poor, black and white, a Great Society, but that is gone now, trampled by this unconscionable war in Vietnam. How can I continue to try and persuade our desperate young men in these despairing ghettos to put down their weapons and embrace non-violence, when their own country is the greatest agent of violence in the world?!

Rapturous APPLAUSE ends in a hollow echo. King freezes. Hoover, LBJ and Humphrey move close to him.

J. EDGAR HOOVER (*triumphant*)   That's it. That's the moment. King drops his mask and reveals the traitor beneath!

VICE PRESIDENT HUMPHREY   He never attacked you personally, Mr. President.

LBJ (*furious*)   *He attacked my policies!*

J. EDGAR HOOVER   "The greatest agent of violence in the world."

LBJ   I've had angry calls all morning from other Movement leaders; Roy Wilkins swears King is being run by the Communists!

VICE PRESIDENT HUMPHREY   That's absurd.

J. EDGAR HOOVER   King's recommendations for the war are exactly the same as those of the American Communist Party!

VICE PRESIDENT HUMPHREY   That doesn't make him a communist!

LBJ   You want to do something useful, Hubert, go talk some sense into Wilbur Mills. Who the hell does King think he is telling me how to handle Vietnam?!

Humphrey leaves. Simultaneously, Bobby Kennedy joins MLK and they shake hands for PHOTOGRAPHERS—freeze on the flash. LBJ studies them coldly.

J. EDGAR HOOVER   He's just like Bobby Kennedy—who loved King's speech, of course. You saw Bobby's comments to the Press?

LBJ   He's workin' himself up for a run. I always knew the two of them would join forces.

J. EDGAR HOOVER   It's what you always suspected.

LBJ   Backstabbing sons of bitches.

King and Bobby exit.

J. EDGAR HOOVER   King has not just betrayed you, Mr. President, he has betrayed the *Country*.

A moment.

LBJ   That program of yours . . .

J. EDGAR HOOVER   COINTELPRO.

LBJ   Set your dogs loose, Jay; everything you got.

J. EDGAR HOOVER   King?

LBJ   Especially King.

LBJ exits. Deke Deloach is immediately at Hoover's elbow. Hoover dictates while Deloach takes notes.

J. EDGAR HOOVER   Formal directive, all departments. As of this day, initiate all our programs to expose, disrupt, misdirect, discredit, or otherwise neutralize all these Black Nationalist Hate organizations, with special attention to Martin Luther King.

> TB: *Montage of surveillance **PHOTOS** of **MLK**. [From this point on, individual **FBI AGENTS** each with a **TAPE RECORDER** should be gradually added to each scene, scattered among the Witness Stands, observing and recording the action.]*

LIGHTS on BOBBY KENNEDY'S SENATE OFFICE. Bobby and his aide, Adam Walinsky. Bobby puts down the phone.

ADAM WALINSKY What? What does LBJ want to see you *about*?

SENATOR BOBBY KENNEDY He wouldn't say. Just that it's important and he wants to talk privately.

ADAM WALINSKY He wants to keep you out of the race.

SENATOR BOBBY KENNEDY It's like what Churchill said about the Germans—he's either at your feet or at your throat.

ADAM WALINSKY He's out of control and he's gonna take the whole country down with him. *You've got to run, Bobby.*

SENATOR BOBBY KENNEDY Adam.

ADAM WALINSKY There's no neutral position here. To stay out of the race is to *support* Johnson's re-election.

SENATOR BOBBY KENNEDY If I run, people will say I'm just doing it out of ambition and envy.

ADAM WALINSKY Fuck what people say! If you don't carry the banner, who will? Humphrey? He's a lapdog. McCarthy? He'll never win. Who else is there?

SENATOR BOBBY KENNEDY What if I run and all I accomplish is splitting the party and electing Nixon? Is that any better?

ADAM WALINSKY You're the best chance the Liberal wing of the party has and don't think for a second that fucker Johnson doesn't know it. That's why he's gunning for you!

LIGHTS shift. OVAL OFFICE. LBJ and Bobby. Beneath the polite banter, both men are very wary.

SENATOR BOBBY KENNEDY   I have to say, it's not what I was expecting. A commission?

LBJ   A blue-ribbon commission to evaluate our policy in Vietnam, soup to nuts.

Beat.

SENATOR BOBBY KENNEDY   It would have to be Independent.

LBJ   Wouldn't be any good if it wasn't. It could bring the country together, heal our differences, and point us towards a real path to peace.

SENATOR BOBBY KENNEDY   And you want me to sit on this?

LBJ   I want you to Chair it.

Beat.

SENATOR BOBBY KENNEDY   Why? Why me?

LBJ   Who better? You were there in the beginning with Jack. Our policy differences are certainly well documented so nobody could accuse you of carryin' water for me. For the record, the Press has always put us up against one another like there was some kind of war there. I never felt that way myself.

SENATOR BOBBY KENNEDY   I've never felt any personal animosity towards you.

LBJ   Exactly.

SENATOR BOBBY KENNEDY   Sometimes you read articles where they say I'm thinking about running just to spite you for petty reasons, or out of my own ambition. None of that is true.

LBJ   You're not thinking of running?

SENATOR BOBBY KENNEDY   If I were to enter the campaign it would be simply because I thought that would be the best way of ending the bloodshed in Vietnam.

LBJ But if this commission accomplished that . . .

SENATOR BOBBY KENNEDY . . . there wouldn't be any need for me to run.

LBJ It would be a great service to your country.

SENATOR BOBBY KENNEDY We would have to have a free hand, to, to call witnesses and review materials.

LBJ Of course.

SENATOR BOBBY KENNEDY And the assurance that our findings would be made public without revision; our conclusions, however unfavorable they might or might not be to your administration, would be unchallenged; and our recommendations followed without argument.

Beat.

LBJ I think you misunderstand me.

SENATOR BOBBY KENNEDY I don't think I do.

LBJ I don't think our system ever contemplated turning over the functions of the Commander in Chief to a civilian commission, and to admit to the world and the enemy and his own country, that he didn't believe in what he was doing.

SENATOR BOBBY KENNEDY I am fully prepared to accept your offer to head this commission under the conditions I have just outlined. But if you can't accept those conditions, then I don't see any point in my participation.

LBJ I think, Senator, we should both do exactly what we feel we have to do.

LIGHTS SHIFT. Kennedy leaves. Hoover enters but LBJ never takes his eyes off Kennedy. Deloach stands nearby, waiting orders.

LBJ King's not the only traitor out there, Jay. There are lots of other people attacking me: Labor, the Press, the Universities—the

Democratic Party. I need to know who I can trust and who I can't. (*staring at Bobby*) That includes Congress.

Hoover nods. LBJ leaves. Deloach consults with Hoover.

J. EDGAR HOOVER Extend our surveillance to all anti-war groups and individuals; *no exceptions*.

Hoover stops Deloach from writing.

That would include, but not be limited to, Senator Bobby Kennedy.

*TB: **Montage of surveillance PHOTOS of Bobby Kennedy.***

LIGHTS SHIFT. PENTAGON, McNamara OFFICE. LBJ/ McNamara. From outside, we can hear PROTESTERS.

PROTESTORS HEY, HEY, LBJ, HOW MANY KIDS DID YOU KILL TODAY! HEY, HEY, LBJ, HOW MANY KIDS DID YOU KILL TODAY! HEY, HEY, LBJ, HOW MANY KIDS DID YOU KILL TODAY! HEY, HEY, LBJ, HOW MANY KIDS DID YOU KILL TODAY!

*While LBJ/McNamara talk, a third man, **NORMAN MORRISON**, stands quietly nearby, holding a can of kerosene. LBJ doesn't see him but McNamara does, he can't take his eyes off Morrison. LBJ glances out the window at the PROTESTORS.*

LBJ (*grim humor*) It's like Fort Apache around here. They're feelin' it up on the Hill, I can tell you that. Even the Senate Majority Leader is after me now to throttle back! Hoover says Tip O'Neil is goin' to come out against the War. Of course, he's holdin' Jack Kennedy's old seat so, no surprise who's pullin' his strings. On the other hand, the Generals and the Senate Hawks want me to "take off the shackles" on our war effort! Everywhere I turn, I'm bein' beaten, pillar to post. Everybody talks about the awesome power of the President. You know what the President is? It's like bein' a jackass in the middle of a hailstorm; all you can do is stand there and take it. (*Beat*) How's your wife, Bob?

McNamara doesn't respond.

NORMAN MORRISON (*quietly to McNamara*) For weeks I had been praying about the deaths of all those children in Vietnam.

LBJ Bob?

NORMAN MORRISON And then this morning, without any warning at all, I was shown what I must do—as clearly as I was shown that night in 1955 that you should be my wife.

ROBERT MCNAMARA My wife?

Morrison kneels down in prayer.

LBJ Are you OK?

ROBERT MCNAMARA They expect to let her leave the hospital soon. (*gallows humor*) My friends say she has my ulcer.

LBJ Anything she needs, you let me know. (*glances out window*) How many people they got for this "March on the Pentagon?"

ROBERT MCNAMARA Justice estimates 22,000; the FBI, closer to 28,000.

Morrison strikes a match.

ROBERT MCNAMARA You smell that?

LBJ What?

ROBERT MCNAMARA Smoke?

LBJ They're probably burning their draft cards out there.

Morrison blows out the match.

LBJ I want all those sons of bitches arrested and prosecuted to the fullest extent of the law!

ROBERT MCNAMARA Strictly speaking that's a matter for the police but yes, I believe they will be aggressive.

LBJ (*re: Protesters*) What do we got for Security?

ROBERT MCNAMARA   Park Police and U.S. Marshals, backed up by 2,000 DC Policemen, 1,700 National Guard Troops and 6,000 active Army soldiers, including elements of the 82nd Airborne.

LBJ   Let'em levitate that.

McNamara looks out the window.

ROBERT MCNAMARA   Norman Morrison burned himself to death right out there.

Morrison rises and stands next to McNamara.

LBJ   That crazy Quaker minister?

ROBERT MCNAMARA   They tried to get the scorch marks off the sidewalk but when the light is at a certain angle you can still see them. He put his baby daughter . . .

He stops; can't recall the name.

NORMAN MORRISON   Emily.

ROBERT MCNAMARA   Put his baby daughter, Emily—on the grass there, folded his coat, and poured a whole can of kerosene over his head. (*Beat*) The flames were fifteen feet high.

LBJ   How you sleepin' these days, Bob?

Morrison walks off.

ROBERT MCNAMARA   I realize the opinions I'm about to share may be incompatible with your own but, I think our present course in South East Asia has become untenable—dangerous to our interests, costly in lives, and unacceptable to the American people. I think we should put a firm limit on current troop levels—no more increases and halt the bombing.

LBJ (*stunned*)   That's really how you feel?

ROBERT MCNAMARA   I haven't, of course, shared these views with anyone else. (*hesitant*) I had a phone call last week. The position of President of the World Bank will become available in August.

LBJ What did you say?

ROBERT MCNAMARA I didn't say anything one way or the other; the appointment is your prerogative but—it appeals to me. Of course, I will stay on at Defense as long as you want me to.

A moment.

LBJ I don't see any point in drawing this out, do you?

McNamara nods and leaves.

PROTESTORS HEY, HEY, LBJ, HOW MANY KIDS DID YOU KILL TODAY! HEY, HEY, LBJ, HOW MANY KIDS DID YOU KILL TODAY! HEY, HEY, LBJ, HOW MANY KIDS DID YOU KILL TODAY!

LIGHTS SHIFT.

LBJ and Ladybird in a car with Driver. Night. LBJ is restless.

TB: ***IMAGES of Washington Mall filled with sleepy protesters.***

LADY BIRD You sure this is safe?

LBJ We'll be fine, Bird.

Beat.

LADY BIRD Are we looking for anything in particular?

LBJ I wanted to see what they look like.

LADY BIRD It's good to get out, anyway. (*glancing around*) They all look so thin. Maybe we ought to send some food over.

LBJ They're not tourists, Bird.

LADY BIRD They're just kids.

LBJ I don't understand why they hate me so much. Don't they realize I'm just like them? I always hated cops when I was a kid. I took off for California when I was a teenager.

LADY BIRD You never told me that!

LBJ (*shrugging*)   Nothin' to be proud of.

LADY BIRD   What happened?

LBJ   After High School I had no future really. No plans at all except to get outta Johnson City as quick as I could. So one day I just hitchhiked to Los Angeles. (*Beat*) When I finally got there, I 'member standin' on the beach in Santa Monica starin' at the ocean, my eyes buggin' out.

LADY BIRD   Like they were on stalks.

She laughs; He doesn't.

LBJ   My daddy was so mad at me.

LADY BIRD   I can imagine.

LBJ   Not that he could offer me anythin' better. Anythin' at all really.

LADY BIRD   What did you do?

LBJ   Whatever I could find. Washed dishes, picked apples. Slept out in parks. Stayed hungry. (*re: the Kids*) I'm not some conformist middle-class personality. They got exactly the wrong idea about who I am. I don't understand why they hate me so much! (*Beat. To Driver*) Better head back.

SHIFT to DC FUNERAL HOME. A flag-draped casket rises with a framed picture of BLACK SAILOR. Sally enters dressed in black. **SALLY'S HUSBAND** *sits beside the coffin, his head in his hands. He never looks up as LBJ and Lady Bird enter.*

SALLY CHILDRESS   Mr. President; Ma'am; it is so good of you to come.

LADY BIRD   Sally, we are so sorry for your loss.

Lady Bird hugs Sally, then goes over and signs the book, leaving LBJ and Sally standing alone by the coffin. A moment.

LBJ   Did you decide on Arlington?

SALLY CHILDRESS   Yes, sir. (*Beat*) We appreciate your help with that. (*Beat*) It's pretty there. Easy to visit. (*Beat*) I think he would've liked it.

A moment.

LBJ   You take as long as you want, Sally. (*Beat*) There's no need to hurry back. Or anything.

SALLY CHILDRESS   I appreciate that, Sir, but . . . (*glances at her Husband*) . . . it's harder to be at home.

LBJ   Whatever you think.

Lady Bird exits. LBJ moves DC. Sally removes her son's picture from the coffin and holds it to her chest, facing the audience. As the coffin descends, Sally's Husband rises, glaring at LBJ and pointing an accusing finger as the LIGHTS SHIFT.

SITUATION ROOM. LBJ, Humphrey, General Wheeler, General Westmoreland, and **CLARK CLIFFORD** (*New Secretary of Defense*) *all watching TV.*

TB: **FEBRUARY, 1968.** *Images from the TET Offensive,* **with NEWSCASTER and CRONKITE VO.**

NEWSCASTER (*TV*)   In violation of a mutually agreed upon cease-fire, Communist forces launched a surprise nationwide attack during the Tet New Year celebrations yesterday. Enemy forces attacked thirty-six provincial capitals and Saigon, and almost took over the American Embassy there. Heavy fighting continues with large casualties on both sides.

WALTER CRONKITE (*TV*)   We have been too often disappointed by the optimism of the American leaders, both in Vietnam and Washington, to have faith any longer in the silver linings they find in the darkest clouds. To say that we are closer to victory today is to believe, in the face of the evidence, the optimists who have been wrong in the past. To suggest we are on the edge of defeat is to yield to unreasonable pessimism. To say that we are mired in stalemate seems the only realistic, yet unsatisfactory, conclusion.

TB: *Close-up of WALTER CRONKITE.*

WALTER CRONKITE *(TV)* But it is increasingly clear to this reporter that the only rational way out then will be to negotiate, not as victors, but as an honorable people who lived up to their pledge to defend democracy, and did the best they could.

TB *reads:* **VIETNAM: 25,826 AMERICAN DEAD. 116,752 WOUNDED.**

Sally exits. LBJ turns TV off.

LBJ Jesus. When you've lost Cronkite, what is there?

GENERAL WHEELER Despite what the press claims, Mr. President, this has actually been a terrible defeat for the North Vietnamese!

LBJ Not according to Walter Cronkite.

GENERAL WHEELER Almost 80,000 men killed. Their offensive capability has been severely degraded.

CLARK CLIFFORD General, I'm new to my position obviously, stepping into some big shoes for Mr. McNamara, but if I may ask, what is the normally accepted ratio of wounded to killed?

GENERAL WESTMORELAND A three to one ratio among the North Vietnamese would be a *conservative* estimate.

CLARK CLIFFORD How many regular soldiers do you think they have left now?

GENERAL WESTMORELAND Perhaps 240,000 men.

CLARK CLIFFORD Well, with 80,000 killed and a wounded ratio of three to one, that makes *320,000 men killed or wounded.* Who the hell is there left for us to be fighting?!

GENERAL WHEELER The goal has always been to force a political settlement—never to achieve a military solution!

CLARK CLIFFORD Then what in the name of God are five hundred thousand American soldiers doing out there? Chasing girls?

This is not a semantic game, General. If the deployment of those men is not an effort to gain a military solution then words have lost all their meaning!

LBJ   What about your last request for 200,000 more men? Will that do the job?

The Generals exchange looks.

GENERAL WHEELER   I can't guarantee that, no.

CLARK CLIFFORD   If 200,000 is insufficient, how many more would be needed?

GENERAL WESTMORELAND   There's no way of knowing for sure, Mr. Secretary.

CLARK CLIFFORD   What about the South Vietnamese army? How much longer must the United States carry the burden of the war?

GENERAL WHEELER   We don't know when, if ever, the South Vietnamese will be ready to shoulder the main burden of fighting.

LBJ   Thank you, gentlemen.

Wheeler and Westmoreland leave.

Clark is obviously shaken.

LBJ   You see what I'm up against, Clark? And even if by some miracle Congress were to OK more troops, we can't fund it; Wilbur Mills is holding up the entire budget, demanding his pound of entitlement flesh before he'll approve any kind of tax increase.

CLARK CLIFFORD   Let me see what I can do on the Defense side, sir.

Clifford leaves. Humphrey enters and hands a document to LBJ.

VICE PRESIDENT HUMPHREY   The polls you asked for, sir. I think these need to be taken with a grain of salt. They show McCarthy doing surprisingly well in the New Hampshire primary. I don't pretend to understand it; the man isn't remotely in your league.

LBJ   They don't believe me anymore, Hubert. "The Credibility Gap." If I said the Sun will rise in the East tomorrow, everybody and his brother would be lookin' West.

VICE PRESIDENT HUMPHREY   I still think you'll win.

LBJ   Hell, even if I beat him, I lose. McCarthy will get at least forty percent 'cause every son of a bitch in New Hampshire who's mad at his wife or the postman or anybody is going to vote for Eugene McCarthy and then the Press will say, "It's a defeat for Johnson!" Then there's Bobby, of course, sittin' on the sidelines, lickin' his chops.

VICE PRESIDENT HUMPHREY   In public he seems genuinely ambivalent about running.

LBJ   Don't you believe that, "Please don't throw me in the briar patch" bullshit! Bobby's lettin' McCarthy test the waters but if he wins tonight, Bobby will jump in with both feet and it'll be, "Fuck you, Eugene!" There will be Kennedys poppin' out of the woodwork all over the country.

Sally Childress enters.

SALLY CHILDRESS   Representative Mills.

LBJ nods; Sally leaves.

VICE PRESIDENT HUMPHREY   You want me to stay?

LBJ shakes his head. Humphrey exits in one direction as Rep. Wilbur Mills enters from the other.

REPRESENTATIVE WILBUR MILLS (*solicitous*)   Mr. President, how are you? Terrible business these days in Vietnam; the burden you have to carry; I don't know how you do it.

LBJ   If you're finished with the hand job, Wilbur, we need this tax bill. Look, I know nothin' in this life comes free, and so in exchange for a ten billion dollar personal and corporate tax increase, I am reluctantly prepared to accept a cut in domestic expenditures of four billion.

A moment.

REPRESENTATIVE WILBUR MILLS   Six billion in cuts.

LBJ   Six?

REPRESENTATIVE WILBUR MILLS   Tough medicine but the economy needs a dose of fiscal restraint.

LBJ   I knew this country doctor once, had an old rancher come in complainin' of a fever, so he dosed him real good with turpentine and the old fella died. "You've killed my husband" the widow cried! The doctor allowed as how that might be but, he said, "He ain't got that fever no more, has he?" Six billion is an overdose of fiscal restraint. Hell, a cut that size could bring on a recession.

REPRESENTATIVE WILBUR MILLS   Six billion.

LBJ   I know we got an election coming up, Wilbur, but even so, responsible men need to step up and do what's right for their country.

REPRESENTATIVE WILBUR MILLS   That's exactly what I'm doing.

LBJ   What you're doin' is holdin' this tax bill for blackmail.

REPRESENTATIVE WILBUR MILLS   For common-damn-sense! The party is over. Somebody has to turn off the porch light, throw the drunks outta the living room, and clean up the mess in the kitchen!

LBJ   You've over-reached, Wilbur and now you're gonna wind up with nothin'!

REPRESENTATIVE WILBUR MILLS   Your mistake, Mr. President, is confusing yourself with the country. Disagreeing with you is not "disloyal," or an "act of treason."

LBJ   You listen to me . . . !

REPRESENTATIVE WILBUR MILLS   . . . No, you listen to me! The time when you could push us all around is OVER! I've got most of the Southern Democrats and ALL of the Republicans in both

Houses. All you've got left is a handful of Northern Democrats and precious few of them after New Hampshire tonight. Ten–six is the offer; now; *today*. But if I walk outta here without a deal, I make no promises about tomorrow.

A moment.

LBJ   Okay.

REPRESENTATIVE WILBUR MILLS   We have a deal? (*silence*) I need to hear the words.

LBJ (*quietly*)   Ten–six.

Mills leaves. LIGHTS SHIFT. WHITE HOUSE. FAMILY ROOM. LBJ & Lady Bird watch TV with election night news from the New Hampshire Primary.

LADY BIRD   It's still a victory, darlin'.

LBJ   Except when the press says it isn't.

LADY BIRD   You didn't personally campaign in New Hampshire, your name wasn't even on the ballot, and you still beat him, honey, forty-nine to forty-two percent!

LBJ   Hell, when you add in the write-in Republican votes McCarthy got, I only beat him by 240 votes overall. "Landslide Lyndon."

LADY BIRD   There's no way around Mills?

LBJ   He's got the whip hand now. They call me, "Master of the Senate." I'm not the Master of a damn thing. I'm the Master of nothing. You should see the hate mail I get now. We had to let Sally go.

LADY BIRD   Sally? No.

LBJ   She couldn't handle it anymore.

LADY BIRD   What will you have to cut?

LBJ It'll be a bloodbath. Poverty. Education. Job Programs. Social Security. Aid to Families with Dependent Children. Hey, poor people don't vote and they sure as hell don't make campaign contributions, so screw'em! I understand the economics but there's a mean-ness here that goes beyond the numbers. When did the Christian thing to do change from helpin' your fallen brother up, to puttin' your heel on his throat?

LADY BIRD What about Dirksen?

LBJ He's lookin' two years down the road at a Republican President. It's the goddamn War, Bird. I knew from the start that if I left the woman I loved—the Great Society—in order to fight this bitch of a war, I'd lose everything.

SOUND of MUSIC. SPOT on **TV ANNOUNCER**.

TV ANNOUNCER And now we bring you a special announcement from Washington!

SPOT on Senator Bobby Kennedy surrounded by jubilant aides and family members.

SENATOR BOBBY KENNEDY First, my congratulations to Eugene McCarthy for his extraordinary showing in New Hampshire! Second—I am announcing today my candidacy for the Presidency of the United States!

SOUNDS of ecstatic crowds. Lady Bird walks off.

SENATOR BOBBY KENNEDY I want to emphasize that my decision reflects no personal animosity or disrespect towards President Johnson, however New Hampshire has revealed profound divisions in the country created by President—uh, created by the *policies of* President Johnson. At stake is not simply leadership of our party, or even our country—it is our right to moral leadership on this planet!

LIGHTS out on Bobby. SPOT on LBJ.

LBJ (*to the audience*) I watched a pack of wolves once take down this old steer. They'd nip him from one side and he'd swing those big horns around, tryin' to get at'em, and maybe he would but mostly he missed and when he missed, another one would bite at him on the other side. They wouldn't go for the throat; not like you'd think. They'd tire him out first. Slow him down. Then go after his legs; tear his hamstrings; bring him down to his knees. They might tear at his throat then but that wouldn't be what they really wanted. They'd want him to bleed so much he can't fight back any more and then they'd go after his guts. They'd chew into his stomach and eat their way through his intestines while he's still alive and can feel everything, feel them chewin' away, tearin' at his heart.

LIGHTS SHIFT. DEAD ARMY, NAVY, and MARINE SERVICEMEN enter and clear the stage.

LBJ wanders through the HALLS of the WHITE HOUSE with a small flashlight in his hand, mumbling to himself. From the DARKNESS, the SERVICEMEN echo his words.

LBJ shuffles stacks of LETTERS in his hands. Some of them fall to the floor unnoticed.

LBJ Dear Mr. and Mrs. Hernandez. I wish to inform. I regret to inform. It is with a heavy heart. As your President, it is with a heavy heart. Your son. I regret to inform you. Lieutenant Joseph B. Hernandez was killed. Dear Mr. and Mrs. Frazer. The United States thanks you for your sacrifice . . .

RED ROOM. LBJ stops in front of a PORTRAIT hanging on the wall. LBJ stares at it intently. A moment.

What? (*Beat*) You know. *You* know. (*Beat*) How did you . . . ? (*Beat*) I can't do that. No.

Lady Bird appears in her bathrobe.

LADY BIRD (*very concerned*) Lyndon? Honey? What are you doin'?

The Soldiers slowly exit but they leave their helmets/hats behind.

LBJ (*re: the picture*) Talkin' to Woody here.

Lady Bird puts her glasses on and is shocked to realize that LBJ is talking to a picture.

LADY BIRD   Woodrow Wilson?

LBJ   Twenty-eighth President of the United States. Inspired Roosevelt's New Deal. Got the country through World War One and won a Nobel Prize for peace. 'Course he didn't have Martin Luther King to compete with.

Lady Bird picks up some of the fallen LETTERS.

LADY BIRD   You dropped some of your papers, Lyndon.

LBJ   Letters. Personal letters. Can't finish'em.

LADY BIRD   Maybe Dick or one of the other speech–writers can help you.

LBJ snatches the LETTERS back.

LBJ   Those are mine! *I write these.* Nobody else.

LADY BIRD   Okay. Okay.

LBJ glances back at the PORTRAIT.

LBJ   Wilson had a stroke in 1919; left him completely *paralyzed*; a living death. His wife secretly ran the government for a year and a half but the Republicans swept to power anyway and the US never joined the League of Nations and all Wilson's dreams died.

LADY BIRD   That's not gonna happen to you.

LBJ   It could! It could. I'm so tired, Bird. All the time. Bone tired. Even my eyes hurt. (*Beat*) My grandma had a paralyzin' stroke and my folks used to make me sit with her. "Keep grandma company." I hated it. Little wizened thing, sittin' there in bed, stiff as a board, starin' into nothin'. String of drool dripping down her chin. Sometimes I would say mean things to her, just to see if I could get a response but she never said nothin' and when I think on it now, I'm so ashamed. Why would I do that?

LADY BIRD   The doctors say you're fine.

LBJ (*great contempt*)   What do they know! All those so-called
"Experts"—I wouldn't give a plug nickle for the lot of 'em! I don't
give a damn 'bout the election, Bird, but if I lose they're gonna cut
my Medicare and my Education and my Poverty programs.

LADY BIRD   The people love you, darlin'.

LBJ   I know they do, I know they do, but the problem, see, the
problem is I been sabotaged in the press. They get on me and get
on me and the people start to wonder; they think I'm wrong about
the War. And then Bobby God-damn Kennedy takes up the Cause
with King on his payroll stirrin' up the Negroes, and then the
Communists step in. The Communists control the networks now!
Did you know that? All three networks. It's all in the FBI reports.

LADY BIRD   I don't think Jay is your friend, Lyndon.

LBJ   He's the only friend I got!

LADY BIRD   *No, he is not!*

   Lady Bird's words seem to reach LBJ, bring him back to the present.

LBJ   We might have a real peace feeler from the North Vietnamese.
Could be fake but Clark Clifford doesn't think so.

LADY BIRD   That's wonderful!

LBJ   I'm ready to talk peace, hell, I been ready, but now the *South
Vietnamese are draggin' their feet!* Can you believe that? After all we
done for them. Jay thinks there's somethin' fishy goin' on there but
I don't know, I don't know. There has just been a—a *panic* in the
last couple of weeks. We need more taxes—in an election year. We
need more troops—in an election year. We need cuts in the domestic
budget—in an election year. And yet I can't tell the people what
they'll get in return for all that sacrifice. I used to know. I had this—
dream about the country. What it could be. And it was right there,
Bird, so close I could almost wrap my arms around it and whatever
it took seemed like such a small thing and so at first you tell yourself,

if you think about it at all, that it's not much of a line to cross—hell, you've done it before, or somethin' like it—maybe even somethin' worse. You tell yourself, hell, everybody does it. And so you lie. And then you gotta cover that one with another one. And then another. Until one day you turn around and you don't know where you are anymore, or who you are, and the dream—is gone. It's all gone. All of it. And all you really know is . . . (*looking at his letters*) . . . I did this. Nobody else. *I did this.* (*a moment of decision*) Maybe—maybe I should quit; not run again.

A moment. They look at one another

LADY BIRD   Well, that would suit the girls just fine. They'd love to have their daddy back.

Beat.

LBJ   And you?

Beat.

LADY BIRD   Yes.

LIGHTS shift abruptly.

TB reads: **MARCH 31, 1968. VIETNAM: 27,589 AMERICAN DEAD. 128,366 WOUNDED.**

OVAL OFFICE. A **BUTLER** *helps LBJ change into his suit as a* **MAID** *helps Lady Bird into her dress while a* **MAKEUP** *person makes last minute adjustments to LBJ's face and nervous* **AIDES** *rush in and out. LBJ sits behind his desk.*

AIDE#1   Ready when you are, Mr. President.

Lady Bird touches LBJ and then steps aside to watch. LBJ nods, AIDE#1 gives the high sign to an offstage TV Executive.

AIDE#1   In Five . . . Four . . . Three . . .

As Aide#1 withdraws, continuing his countdown, lights dim. LBJ is now very calm and collected.

126

LBJ   Tonight, I want to speak to you of peace in Southeast Asia. I am unilaterally ordering a cessation of bombing and am ready to send negotiators to Paris to discuss the means of bringing this ugly war to an end. The strength of America lies in the unity of our people but there is deep division in our country. For my part, I feel strongly that I should not permit the Presidency to become involved in the partisan divisions that are developing in this political year. With America's sons in the fields far away, with America's future under challenge right here at home, with our hopes and the world's hopes in the balance every day, I do not believe I should devote an hour or a day of my time to any personal partisan causes or to any duties other than the awesome duties of this office—the Presidency of your country. Accordingly, I shall not seek, and I will not accept the nomination of my party for another term as your President!

LIGHT SHIFT. Humphrey enters; he is stunned.

VICE PRESIDENT HUMPHREY   I don't know what to say, Mr. President.

LBJ   Well, that's a first right there! It's all yours, Hubert. (*whispers*) Now, go beat that son of a bitch.

VICE PRESIDENT HUMPHREY (*giddy*)   Which one?

LBJ   All of 'em, Hubert! BEAT ALL OF 'EM.

LIGHTS SHIFT. WHITE HOUSE. DAY.

TB reads: **NINE MONTHS LATER. DECEMBER, 1968. VIETNAM: 38,620 AMERICAN DEAD. 192,616 WOUNDED.**

LBJ is joined in the Oval Office by Lady Bird, Richard Nixon, and **PAT NIXON**. *In a half-light SL, Bobby watches, while in a half-light SR, MLK watches.*

PAT NIXON   Oh, my, you've done such a lovely job, Lady Bird.

LADY BIRD   That's very sweet of you, Pat, but most of the credit goes to Jackie, of course. I think the hardest things to deal with are the security issues, especially with teenagers. They really do hate it. But I guess you're familiar with that.

PAT NIXON   Like living in a fishbowl.

LADY BIRD   And the noise. You go to sleep with the protests and then you wake up to it. The ranch has been such a blessing. Let me show you the girl's rooms.

Lady Bird and Pat leave. A moment.

RICHARD NIXON (*re: the women*)   How'd we get so lucky, huh? In college, Pat wouldn't have anything to do with me at first. I used to drive her and her dates around like a chauffeur, just to get close to her. Wore her resistance down eventually. Not the usual courtship but effective.

LBJ   Drink?

RICHARD NIXON   Sure. Thought you were on the wagon?

LBJ   I quit a year into my second term; didn't want anything to cloud my judgement but now I'm a free man. Almost.

RICHARD NIXON   And what will you do when you go back to your ranch?

LBJ   I'm gonna have a cigarette. And I'm gonna wrap my arms around Walter Jenkins.

A moment.

RICHARD NIXON   You look great, Mr. President.

LBJ   Thank you. Mr. President.

RICHARD NIXON (*smiling*)   Not yet. Not yet. President elect.

LBJ gestures towards the desk.

LBJ   Want to try her out?

RICHARD NIXON   I don't know.

LBJ   Go ahead.

Nixon sits behind the desk, savoring the experience.

RICHARD NIXON   Ike used to make me wait, standing there in the corner like a school boy, before he would finally deign to recognize my presence.

LBJ   Jack was the same way.

RICHARD NIXON   And look at us now, huh?

A moment.

RICHARD NIXON   A helluva year. Dr. King's death.

SPOT on MLK.

LBJ   Yes.

RICHARD NIXON   Tragic. Congress did at least restore most of your Poverty Funds afterwards. How come you didn't go to his funeral?

LBJ   Security.

MLK *(calling over his shoulder)*   Get out here, Ralph, you're missin' the sunset! *(facing out)* Ben, make sure you play, "Take My Hand Precious Lord," in the meeting tonight! Play it real pretty.

SPOT on MLK goes off, leaving him in the dark.

RICHARD NIXON *(shaking his head)*   And then Bobby. What a shock.

SPOT on Bobby

LBJ   Bobby.

SENATOR BOBBY KENNEDY *(addressing crowd)*   I hope now that the California primary is over, we can have a debate on what direction we want this country to go. What we're going to do with those who still suffer with hunger in this country. With poverty. And about our policies which have been so unsuccessful in Vietnam. And so, I thank all of you who made this possible, and on to Chicago and let's win there!

LBJ   He'd of beaten you.

RICHARD NIXON   Maybe. Would that have made you feel better? Or worse?

LBJ   Two weeks before the election, I found out that you were spiking the Paris Peace Talks.

RICHARD NIXON   Now, wait a minute . . .

LBJ   . . . Secretly telling the South Vietnamese government NOT to make a deal *now* because you would make them a better deal after you got elected . . .

RICHARD NIXON   . . . Mr. President, that's just ridiculous . . . .

LBJ   . . . prolongin' the war for months, maybe for years, just to gain political advantage in the election. Some people would call that TREASON! So, I took that information to Hubert and I said, "What do you want to do?" He was only a point or two behind you in the polls then and closin' fast and you know what he told me? Hubert said, "Well, if I go public with it and I win, then everybody will always say I only beat Nixon because of that. And if I go public with it and I lose, Nixon won't be able to govern because half the country will hate his guts." So, he told me not to do anythin'.

RICHARD NIXON   He's a good man, Humphrey.

LBJ   Yes, he is.

RICHARD NIXON (*gesturing to room*)   Too good for this, really.

LBJ   How do you sleep at night?

A moment.

RICHARD NIXON   Why didn't you go public? With whatever you think you had. I'm just guessing here, but whatever information you think you recovered, did you acquire that, maybe, by illegally wiretapping my campaign? And illegally wiretapping the offices of our allies, the South Vietnamese government? To answer your question, I sleep very well at night and for the same reason you do; I know what it takes to get here and I'm willing to pay that price.

LBJ   And what are you going to do now that you are here?

RICHARD NIXON   The same thing as you, Mr. President; I'm going to change this country. I'm going to make it great again.

LBJ   Get the hell away from my desk, you son of a bitch.

Nixon rises. Lady Bird and Pat Nixon return. Nixon moves to Pat and she takes his arm. Together, they begin to process up the center of the stage towards an elevated platform where Hoover, a toad-like Cardinal Richelieu, waits for them.

The rest of the **COMPANY** *assembles in the Witness Boxes and as Nixon and Pat pass by, they murmur respectfully . . .*

COMPANY   Mr. President. Mr. President. Mr. President.

LBJ and Lady Bird watch from the side of the stage. LBJ lights a cigarette and inhales gratefully.

Pat stops a step below the platform so that Nixon stands alone on top, beside a beaming Hoover.

LBJ exhales a cloud of smoke.

LBJ   Let's go home, Bird.

Nixon throws his arms in the air, both hands displaying his signature "V" for "Victory" sign. Everyone freezes on stage.

BLACKOUT.

END OF PLAY

ACKNOWLEDGMENTS

Many people made this play possible. The original impulse was of course, the American Revolutions Project at the Oregon Shakespeare Festival which commissioned and produced *All the Way*, the first LBJ play. *The Great Society* was subsequently commissioned by the Seattle Repertory Theatre under the leadership of Jerry Manning and Braden Abraham. It was developed during residencies at the Orchard Project and the MacDowell Colony and in workshops at the OSF and Seattle Rep. Numerous people generously shared their knowledge and analysis of the underlying events, among them: Doris Kearns Goodwin, Joe Califano, Jr., Bob Moses, and Mark Updegrove and the LBJ library staff. The LBJ family was very generous with their time and support. The joint world premiere was shared by the SRT and OSF and the play was directed by Bill Rauch and my dramaturg was Tom Bryant, both longtime colleagues and dear friends. There are too many artists, designers, and technicians to acknowledge here but I want to single out Jack Willis who originated the role of LBJ in both plays. My agent, Derek Zasky at WME, did a superb job and I am, as always, especially grateful for the support of my family, especially Sarah, Joshua, and Deborah McDermott, aka, "the Greek Goddess."

"Panoramic, instructive, and generally enthralling . . . forcefully evokes a tumultuous era, one (as Schenkkan pointedly reminds us) that set the stage for our current political and social landscape."—*Seattle Times*

The tumultuous beginning of Lyndon B. Johnson's presidency that Robert Schenkkan presented in the multiple Tony Award-winning *All the Way* continues in *The Great Society*. The play had its world premiere at the Oregon Shakespeare Festival in July 2014, directed by Bill Rauch and starring Jack Willis, and ran at the Seattle Repertory Theatre. In the years from 1965 to 1968, LBJ struggles to fight a "war on poverty" even as his war in Vietnam spins out of control. Besieged by political opponents, Johnson marshals all his political wiles to try to pass some of the most important social programs in U.S. history, while the country descends into chaos over the war and backlash against civil rights. In the tradition of the great multi-part Shakespearean historical plays, *The Great Society* is an unflinching examination of the morality of power.

"*The Great Society* continues a profound and searching engagement with a key era of recent U.S. history . . . moves at top speed, hurtling onwards . . . it all works brilliantly."
—*Portland Theatre Scene*

"Speaks powerfully to today through the politics of yesterday . . . A taut political thriller . . . Schenkkan's writing shines as he crafts potent drama . . . A vital study for all those who wish to learn from the past in order to gain some idea of what we might do in the present."—*American-Statesman*, Austin 360

"Engrossing . . . A monumental achievement . . . genius . . . A great play."
—*Queen Anne News*

ROBERT SCHENKKAN is a Pulitzer Prize-, Tony Award-, and Writers Guild Award-winning author of stage, television, and film. He has been nominated for two Emmys and is the author of twelve original full-length plays, two musicals, and a collection of one-act plays. He cowrote the feature film *The Quiet American*, and his television credits include *The Pacific*, *The Andromeda Strain*, and *Spartacus*.

Author photograph by Andrea J. Walker

GROVE PRESS
an imprint of Grove Atlantic
Distributed by Publishers Group West

groveatlantic.com   PRINTED IN THE USA

DRAMA $16.00
ISBN 978-0-8021-2373-2
51600

9 780802 123732